THINKING THROUGH DEATH

Volume I

SCOTT KRAMER

Spokane Community College

KUANG-MING WU

University of Wisconsin-Oshkosh

ROBERT E. KRIEGER PUBLISHING COMPANY
MALABAR, FLORIDA
1988

Original Edition 1988

Printed and Published by
ROBERT E. KRIEGER PUBLISHING COMPANY, INC.
KRIEGER DRIVE
MALABAR, FLORIDA 32950

LIBRARY OF CONGRESS
Library of Congress Cataloging-in-Publication Data

Thinking through death / [compiled by] Scott Kramer, Kuang-ming Wu.
 p. cm.
 ISBN 0-89464-220-0 (Volume I Cloth)
 ISBN 0-89464-337-1 (Volume I Paper)
 ISBN 0-89464-294-4 (Volume II Cloth)
 ISBN 0-89464-338-X (Volume II Paper)
 1. Death. I. Kramer, Scott. II. Wu, Kuang-ming.
BD444.T555 1988
128'.5—dc19   87-29019
                                                                   CIP

10 9 8 7 6 5 4 3 2

For Bernard Kramer, Judi, and Yung-show Wu

Table of Contents

Volume I

Volume II

Acknowledgments

We would like to thank Professor J. D. Ellsworth of the University of Hawaii, and Professor Joan Stambaugh of Hunter College for their original contributions to this book.

We are also indebted to Wen-yen Wu, Roberta Kramer and Elaine S. Rudd for their assistance in the preparation and editing of this manuscript.

We are grateful to the following for permission to reprint previously published material.

Jonathan Barnes, ed. *The Complete Works of Aristotle: The Revised Oxford Translation*, Vols. One and Two, Bollingen Series 71:2. Copyright © 1984 by the Jowett Copyright Trustees. Published by Princeton University Press. Excerpts, Vol. 1, pp. 745, 751, 760–1, and Vol. 1, pp. 740–743, reprinted with permission of Princeton University Press.

Reprinted from *The Dialogues of Plato* translated by Benjamin Jowett (4th ed. 1953) by permission of Oxford University Press.

Anthology of Chinese Literature, Burton Watson (tr.) in Cyril Birch (ed.). © 1965 by Grove Press, Inc. Reprinted by arrangement with Grove Press, Inc.

Wing-Tsit Chan, trans., *A Source Book in Chinese Philosophy* Copyright © 1963 by Princeton University Press. Excerpts reprinted with permission of Princeton University Press.

From The Complete Works of Chuang Tzu, tr. by Burton Watson, 1968. Reprinted by permission of Columbia University Press.

Basic Writings of Hsun Tzu, tr. by Burton Watson, 1967. Reprinted by permission of Columbia University Press.

From *The Tibetan Book of the Dead, or the After-Death Experiences on the Bardo Plane*, according to Lama Kazi Dawa Samdup's English Rendering, edited by W. Y. Evans-Wenz. Copyright © 1960 by W. Y. Evans-Wentz. Reprinted by permission of Oxford University Press.

From *The Tibetan Book of the Dead* Trans. Francesca Fremantle and Chogyam Trungpa © 1975. Reprinted by arrangement with Shambhala Publications, Inc., 300 Massachusetts Ave., Boston, MA 02115.

Swampland Flowers: The Letters and Lectures of Zen Master Ta Hui, © 1977 by Christopher Cleary. Reprinted by permission of Grove Press, Inc.

Viking Penguin Inc. All rights reserved. Reprinted by permission of Viking Penguin, Inc.

Reprinted from *Searchings* by Gabriel Marcel. English translation © 1967 by Newman/Paulist Press. Originally published in German by Verlag Josef Enecht. Used by permission of Paulist Press.

Excerpt from *Creative Fidelity* by Gabriel Marcel. Copyright © 1964 by Farrar, Strauss and Company. Reprinted by permission of Farrar, Straus and Giroux, Inc.

From *Tractatus Logico-Philosophicus* Ludwig Wittgenstein, with permission of Routledge & Kegan Paul Plc, 1967—sections 6.4–7. and Humanities Press International, Inc., Atlantic Highlands, New Jersey.

Being and Time by Martin Heidegger, translated by Professor Joan Stambaugh, Hunter College, New York, New York.

Jean-Paul Sartre *Being and Nothingness*, tr. by Hazel Barnes. New York: The Philosophical Library 1956).

The Myth of Sisyphus and Other Essays by Albert Camus, translated by Justin O'Brien. Reprinted with permission of Alfred Knopf, Inc. 1955.

Reprinted with permission of Macmillan Publishing Company and SCM Press Ltd. *New Essays in Philosophical Theology,* Edited by Antony Flew and Alasdair MacIntyre. Copyright 1955 by Antony Flew and Alasdiar MacIntyre, renewed 1963.

Reprinted from *The Logic of Perfection* by Charles Hartshorne by permission of the The Open Court Publishing Company, La Salle, IL. Reprinted with permission of Open Court Publishing Company, 1962.

From *God and The Soul* by Peter Geach. Reprinted with permission of Routledge & Kegan Paul Plc 1969.

Proceedings of the Society for Psychical Research, Vol. L, Part 182. January 1953 pp. 1–25 Selection "Personal Survival and the Idea of Another World." H. H. Price. (Periodical)

From Paul Ricoeur *Freedom and Nature* with permission of Northwestern University Press, 1966.

Mortal Questions, Thomas Nagel, Cambridge: Cambridge University Press, 1979. Reprinted with permission of Cambridge University Press.

Reprinted by permission of the publishers from *Philosophical Explanations* by Robert Nozick, Cambridge, Massachusetts: Harvard University Press, © 1981 by Robert Nozick.

From *Spirit in Ashes: Hegel, Heidegger and Man-made Mass Death* by Edith Wyschogrod. Reprinted with permission of Yale University Press, 1985.

Introduction

This anthology brings together, for the first time, major philosophers as they think through the meaning of death. The following pages contain the most representative, diverse, penetrating, and readable thoughts on death available anywhere in a two volume collection. These writings furnish a rich variety of Eastern and Western philosophical literature which spans ancient recorded human history through the present.

This anthology is a thinking through death, a philosophizing about death. Thus, the meaning of the terms "philosophy" and "death" should be clarified in order to understand what is in this book.

First, although this work is applicable to the following fields, this anthology is not sociological, literary, psychological, medical, anthropological, religious or historical. It is a *philosophical* anthology on death.

"Philosophy" is thinking at its most coherent, comprehensive, and fundamental level, a serious "thinking through." We have incorporated only philosophical essays here for a simple reason. It is the philosophical approach to death that provides the essential foundation for understanding, classifying, and interpreting various modes of dying. It is thinking through in this basic philosophical sense that develops alternative perspectives, evaluates theoretical solutions, and offers different ethical standards for dealing with death. Reading and thinking along with these great philosophers about the nature of death is the best possible introduction to our own probings of this basic eternal issue, and such probings will decisively help us find a solid frame of reference, and the resources, for dealing with the concrete sociopsychological issues brought about by the various modes of dying.

Secondly, this anthology thinks through *death itself*—not the various modes of dying. Recently we have been inundated with a wealth of anthologies dealing with concrete problems arising from the many ways of dying—anthologies on medical ethics, thanatology, sociology, cultural anthropology, psychology of grieving, and religion—but to date there has been no anthology dealing with death on a *philosophical,* that is, basic, comprehensive level. All this impressive mushrooming of literature on the concrete problems of dying—euthanasia, old age, abortion, infanticide—indicates the urgent importance of the problems of dying without, alas, a clear understanding of what *death itself* is. They badly need a rigorous exploration of what it means to die—a "thinking through" which undercuts all other considerations, and provides a context, a rationale, for various alternative perspectives. So much talk, so little serenity, much less perspective—because we do not *think through* death itself as thoroughly as the great philosophers have done.

Nothing is more natural than to apply a basic universal thinking (philosophy) to a basic universal fact (death). Not surprisingly, many philosophers, classical and contemporary, have thought about death, many schools of philosophy and world religions have arisen out of it, yet curiously nothing is less thought through by most people than the concept of death.

And naturally so. If life is precious to everyone alive, death is a matter of serious concern because death ends life, and thereby makes life seem more precious than if there were no death. Living is what makes all our valuations possible, and death cuts all our values. As we value life above all because life enables all our enjoyments (born of our valuations), so we despise death which destroys all our valuations and enjoyments. Death is abhorrently serious. It is serious because it ends life, and the ending happens universally and irreversibly. Death is abhorrently serious because, despite our wishes to the contrary, our life leads itself inexorably to death, and there is nothing we can do about it. Such a situation naturally breeds intense fear, anxiety, revulsion, and sorrow.

Greek mythology tells of a time when each individual had advanced knowledge of how and when he would die (see Plato's *Gorgias* in Chapter 1). People were so preoccupied with their own deaths that they were frozen, miserable, and ineffectual. Zeus ordered Prometheus to take this knowledge from us, and ever since that time we turn away in revulsion from thinking about death, but, instinctively feeling the importance of death, we are also fascinated at the great philosophers as they think through death.

And what a fascination it is! Nothing is more serious, more urgent, more basic, more concrete, more philosophical, and more paradoxical than our relation to death. The paradox of death—knowledge forbidden yet forever fascinating, philosophically intriguing yet commonly avoided—is at the very heart and nerve of our lives.

One of the purposive desires of conscious life is to know, and all knowledge is within the ken of life. The Socratic injunction of self-knowledge includes the limits of knowledge, and one of these limits is death. Life has within it a death which we cannot know, and this is not a matter for indifference, because without knowing this life-limit our knowledge can never be complete. We cannot help but be concerned about our death, yet we are forbidden to know it. We cannot afford to know death well (we will be miserable and ineffective), and we cannot afford not to know death well (we will be without perspective and orientation for our living).

As our knowledge is delimited by the paradox of death, all other aspects of our lives—emotional, volitional, managerial—are surrounded by frustrating ambiguities and uncertainties. An unexamined death makes for an unexamined life, which is not worth living. How we interpret death provides us a perspective on what life is; how we understand death determines how we should live.

We may feel uneasy when Camus starts his *Myth of Sisyphus* (see Chapter 5) by saying, "There is but one truly serious philosophical problem, and that is suicide." Most of us, however, would agree that death is something ultimately serious in life, if not its ultimate problem. But then, pondering such an "ultimate" in our lives reflects on the quality of the life we lead. Our thinking through death may even give us something ultimately serene to lean on as we live on; and if our ponderings do not give us *the* solution to death, we are perhaps wiser, more comforted, and more aware of life as a result of our investigation. We can live in our discernment of life's true bearing. We can live in perspective, even in confidence (if not strange joy) in our daily dealings.

Camus went on to say, "Judging whether life is or is not worth living amounts to answering the fundamental question of philosophy. All the rest—whether or not the world has three dimensions, whether the mind has nine or twelve categories—comes afterwards." We say (without disagreeing with him, but cutting deeper) that thinking through death amounts to dealing with life's fundamental seriousness. All the rest—whether life is worth living, happiness worth having, or right actions worth doing—comes afterwards, and is given a coherent context for consideration.

Thinking through death with the great philosophers helps us to understand our own deaths—and puts us at ease in our living. For, to turn Confucius around, how is it possible to understand life without understanding death? This is why we offer this anthology.

This book has six chapters, three in each volume. The chapters in volume one are: (1) ancient Greek philosophy; (2) ancient Oriental philosophies; (3) Stoics, Epicureans, Christians, and skeptics. Volume two contains chapters; (4) modern philosophy; (5) nineteenth and early twentieth century philosophy; and (6) contemporary philosophy.

The ordering principle behind this anthology is primarily, although not exclusively, chronological. On the whole, the chapters themselves and the readings within each chapter are arranged from the earliest thoughts on death to the most contemporary. In volume one, however, Chapters 1 and 2 are co-temporal; dealing first with Western, then Eastern ancient philosophies on death, and Chapter 3 consists of four groupings which we believe will render the readings more intelligible.

Each chapter begins with an introduction that sets the stage, highlights the key points, elucidates their significance, and discusses the interrelationships among the various selections. For the most part, however, we let these great thinkers speak for themselves—cogently and relevantly—to the reader today.

The greatest difficulty in compiling an anthology of this nature is the overabundance of philosophical works on death. Out of these writings we have attempted to present the widest possible philosophical perspectives about death. We welcome comments and suggestions from our readers.

Scott Kramer
Kuang-ming Wu

CHAPTER 1
Greek Thought on Death:
An Overview

Recent archeological findings, including the splendid tholos tombs of Mycenae, bear silent witness to the burial customs honored by the earliest Greek-speaking peoples. Valued possessions were buried with the deceased; jars containing wine, oil, and grain have been found in these ancient burial chambers, usually near the sarcophagus. Shards of pottery located by the door, both on the inside and the outside of the tombs, seem to indicate that the Greeks shared a final toast to the dead, sealed the tomb, then toasted the dead again, perhaps at some later time. Goods and possessions buried with the dead were thought to be needed for a journey into the afterlife.

Besides inhumation, cremation was accepted as a practical way to send the dead on their journey, especially in the Homeric era, when Greeks were dying on foreign soil. As evidenced by their art, literature, and archeological remains, the concept of death was never very far from their thoughts; and, with a few exceptions, they did not hold the belief that death was the end of life.

In the span of two short centuries, the Pythagoreans, Heraclitus, Empedocles, Democritus, Plato, and Aristotle, developed philosophies which would provide the foundation for all subsequent Western thinking through death.

The earliest recorded Greek speculations about death, however, are to be found in their "mythology." Orpheus and Odysseus are the only two major figures who visited the world of Hades (death), and returned, while still alive. Each represents a set of metaphors around which various expressions of death coalesced. These metaphors have come to be known respectively as the Orphic and Homeric myths, and they provide the background out of which Greek philosophy evolved.

The Orphic myths first stated the central feature of almost all subsequent Greek thought about death, metempsychosis—the idea that the soul survives the body. This is evident throughout the recorded Orphic lore; "Undying death" is spoken of on several occasions, the poems tell of a punishment in the Underworld, occasionally of a reward

5

in the "Nether World," and they speak of the body as a prison for the soul. These ideas are the foundations from which a Pythagorean philosophy of death evolved. Furthermore, this view is so natural and fundamental that is it shared by some Hindus, Tibetan Buddhists, and Shintoists (see Chapter 2).

The other great figure in Greek literature to cross into the land of the dead, while still alive, was Odysseus. Throughout the Homeric poems, the *Iliad* and the *Odyssey*, death is always thought of as a transitional phase, a passing of the soul from this world to the next. In the very first lines of the *Iliad* we are told that when death occurs the soul goes to Hades, while the corpse may become spoil for dogs and birds. But it is in the *Odyssey* that Homer provides his clearest description of the place and the condition of these souls.

In book eleven of the *Odyssey* Homer portrays the lost shades in Hades as being mere shadows of the men and women they were on earth. Odysseus speaks to the soul of his dead mother, and although he tries to embrace her, she flits from his arms "like a shadow or a dream." (207) She tells him that "as soon as life leaves the white bones, . . . the spirit, like a dream, flits away, and hovers to and fro." (221-2) Even the wise Teiresias speaks of Hades as a region where there "is no joy," (95) and every soul that Odysseus encounters verifies this, but none more dramatically than Achilles: "Nay, seek not to speak soothingly to me of death, glorious Odysseus. I should choose, as I might live on earth, to serve as the hireling of another, of some portionless man whose livelihood was but small, rather than be lord over all the dead that have perished." (488-92)

The Homeric view of the afterlife is primarily negative; all souls seem to wind up in the same condition regardless of their deeds on earth, there are no apparent rewards for those who exemplified the noblest virtue of the age—courage—and there are no rites of purification. Centuries later Plato would find these concepts totally unacceptable. By rigorously criticizing these views throughout the Dialogues, Plato will attempt to transform the afterlife into something more positive; a place where all souls do not serve under the same conditions, where good lives on earth are rewarded for exemplifying the virtues and bad lives on earth are punished for their vice, and the pursuit of wisdom and knowledge is vital to the purification of the soul. Some of these ideas are as old as the Orphic myths, while others will be borrowed from the Pythagoreans.

The Pythagoreans were the first group of philosophers to study the soul and contemplate the nature of human death. Pythagoras himself left no written works, yet scholars have been able to piece together the writings of Ion of Chios, Xenophanes, Herodotus, Philolaus, Archytas, and others, in order to identify a body of knowledge and beliefs that has come to be known as Pythagoreanism. The central features of their philosophy of death are: (1) transmigration of the soul (attested to in the fragment from Xenophanes of Colophon, a contemporary of Pythagoras); (2) the soul participates in a cycle of reincarnation as animal, plant or human, death is seen as an end to one cycle and the beginning of another (Buddhists regard this as the abominable rounds of rebirths and redeaths against which they produced the ideal of Nirvana; cf. Chapter 2); (3) the belief that all nature is akin, and therefore all life is sacred; (4) the development of an elaborate system of purification for the soul which included various religious rites, vegetarianism, and most important, the acquisition of knowledge; and, finally, (5) the belief that the soul could enjoy a blissful existence after death (as the fragment from Ion of Chios explains), or suffer punishments in the cycle of reincarnation (according to Philolaus). All of the pre-Socratic fragments reprinted below follow the traditional numbering found in Diels-Kranz, and are newly translated by Professor J. D. Ellsworth.

Heraclitus (fl. 500 B.C.) speaks of death in a paradoxical and often cryptic manner. The eleven fragments that we have reprinted in this chapter represent his most interesting thoughts on the nature of death. There is virtually no agreement among scholars as to whether Heraclitus believed in the immortality of the human soul, and posthumous punishments (as fragments 27, 62, 63, and 136 seem to indicate) or whether his strong metaphysical belief—that all reality is in a constant state of change—precludes any serious considerations about immortality (as fragments 36, 77, and 88 seem to indicate).

Empedocles (fl. 450 B.C.) suggests that the mixing of the Elements accounts for human existence (fragments 8, 9, and 35), that nothing is really created or destroyed (fragments 9, 11, and 125), and that reincarnation is a definite possibility (fragment 117). Aetius (first or second century A.D.) recorded Empedocles' view that sleep resulted from a cooling of the blood, that death ensued when all heat had left the body, and that death may be common to both body and soul. The first five fragments are from a verse called *On Nature*, the remaining four verses are from *Katharmoi* (Purifications).

Democritus (fl. 420 B.C.) represents a continuation of Greek thought beginning with Anaximenes and extending through Aristotle, which saw the interconnectedness of air and breath to life and death. Democritus also foreshadows the teachings of Epicurus; both believed that the individual soul is dispersed at death and that man's fear of death is foolish (fragments 199, 203, 205, and 297). The Buddhists, Epicurus, and the early Stoics seem to meet at fragment 189. Democritus and Leucippus claimed that life is maintained by breathing, and that air itself is composed of tiny soul-atoms. This accounts for the popular theory (found in Plato's *Phaedo,* and Aristotle's *On Respiration*) that the soul leaves the body at the time of the last breath.

Plato was familiar with the Homeric myths, the Orphic legends, and Pythagorean philosophy. Therefore it is not surprising to see him develop and expand the concepts of transmigration, judgments in the Afterlife, and purification rites, while rejecting the Homeric concept of death.

We begin with two selections from the *Apology.* In the first passage (29a-b), Socrates admits that he does not know what death is, and states that to fear what one does not understand is the height of folly and ignorance. The second passage (40c-42a) ends the *Apology.* Having been sentenced to death for impiety and corrupting the youth of Athens, Socrates confronts his own death by entertaining two ideas; either death is annihilation, or it is the beginning of the soul's journey into another form of life. These two concepts of death will be discussed by philosophers for many years to come. The translations for all the Platonic Dialogues are by Benjamin Jowett (fourth edition).

The selections from the *Phaedo* are divided into three parts. In the first passage (63b-69e) Socrates and Simmias discuss the belief that the philosophic life purifies the soul, and thus prepares it for the journey into the next world. The second passage (69e-72e) finds Socrates arguing against the popular belief, put forward by Cebes, that the soul is dissipated when the body dies. In the last passage (115a-118a) Socrates confronts his own death with a calm, peaceful, and philosophic composure that completes the picture of how the philosopher ought to live and die.

In the *Gorgias* we find the first of three myths dealing with the judgment of souls in the afterlife. It is interesting to note that this passage (523a-527e) omits an important feature found in Plato's other great eschatological myths (*Republic* and *Phaedrus*), namely the doctrine of reincarnation. In this passage, Socrates, speaking to Polus, Gorgias, and Callicles, expresses his belief that the soul receives a fair trial at the hands of unerring judges, that good souls are rewarded for their goodness, and evil souls are punished for their wickedness.

The next selection is taken from Plato's *Republic* (614b-621d). In this dialogue, Socrates has argued that the soul is immortal, that brave, well-trained soldiers ought not fear death, and that both good and evil take root in the soul, thereby accompanying the soul on its journey into the afterlife. In the "myth of Er," which ends the *Republic,* Socrates tells the story of a brave warrior, Er, who has been killed on the battlefield. Er's soul is allowed to see the afterlife and report his observations to the living. This myth has several interesting features. Like the *Gorgias*, it speaks of a judgment, rewards, and punishments, but it goes much further than that. In this myth, Plato is attempting to correct the Homeric conception of death. Rather than finding all souls miserably lamenting in Hades regardless of their deeds on earth, the "myth of Er" presents a universe which is guided by reason and necessity, so that the study of justice, wisdom, courage, and philosophy can actually purify the human soul. This myth also introduces the Pythagorean doctrine of transmigration. Er watches some very famous souls choose their next life; some will return to earth as humans, others as animals.

The excerpt from the *Phaedrus* (245c-250c) begins with an argument that the soul, being a first principle of self-motion, is immortal and imperishable. Next, Socrates likens the soul to a team of winged steeds and their winged charioteer. While the soul has wings, it is able to soar with the gods to a place beyond the heavens where Beauty and Knowledge are to be seen in their pure form. As the soul sheds its wings and attaches itself to a body it loses its divine vision, and it is forced to feed on semblance rather than ambrosia. This journey is described as a cycle which recurs every ten thousand years, except in the soul of the philosopher who is able to regain his wings after three thousand years.

This myth echoes the Orphic belief that the body is a prison for the soul. It adds to this the Pythagorean elements of a triparte, transmigrating soul. The result is a truly philosophical myth which Plato can use to explain the "doctrine of recollection," the theory of Forms, and the rewards of a philosophical life.

We turn next to a brief selection from Plato's *Meno* (81a-d). After discussing what virtue is, and whether or not virtue is teachable, Socrates and Meno have reached a problem in their argument. How is it possible, asks Meno, to inquire about that which we do not know; and furthermore, if we should discover it, how do we know that we have reached the object of our search? To answer these questions Socrates tells Meno what he has heard from the priests and priestesses, that is; the soul is immortal, death is a transitional phase, all nature is akin (as the Pythagoreans believed), and all knowledge is recollection. The quotation cited by Socrates is from Pindar (fr. 133).

In the *Timaeus* Plato sets forth his account of the origin of the universe. God (the Demiurge) created all other gods (e.g. Zeus and Hera), and entrusted to them the creation of mortal men and animals. The gods themselves are said to be "not altogether immortal and indissoluble," but retain their immortality on the basis of the will of the

Demiurge, who also is responsible for sowing the seed of immortality (the soul) in mortal men. This passage will provide St. Augustine with the philosophical justification for his views on death (see Chapter 3).

Finally, in the *Laws*, one of Plato's last dialogues, we find the Athenian Stranger concerned with the more practical aspects of human death; burial, monuments, ceremonies, etc. The passage indicates that Plato has not, however, given up the belief that the essence of man is his soul, and that the good man has nothing to fear from death.

Aristotle's approach to the philosophy of death differs from Plato's writings in style as well as in content. Whereas Plato's thoughts about death emphasized the Orphic, Homeric, and Pythagorean tradition centering around the soul, the afterlife, and the concepts of rewards and punishments; Aristotle, on the other hand, develops the "scientific" lines of thought first expressed by Empedocles and Democritus.

Aristotle was an acute observer of nature, and nature told him that where there was warmth and moisture there was life; where there was coldness and dryness there was death. Aristotle explains that life and death are bound up with respiration, that death is always due to some lack of heat, and that old age is a process by which the body comes to grow cold and dry.

The two treatises reprinted below are from *The Complete Works of Aristotle.*

References

Aristotle, *The Complete Works of Aristotle: The Revised Oxford Translation.* Vols. one and two. Jonathan Barnes, ed., tr. by G.R.T. Ross. Princeton: Princeton University Press, 1984.

Goold, G. P. et al. eds. *Homer with an English Translation. The Odyssey.* Vol. 1, tr. by A. T. Murray. Cambridge: Harvard University Press, 1976.

Diels, Hermann von and Walter von Kranz *Die Fragmente der Vorsokratiker; Griechisch und Deutsch.* 3 vols. Berlin: 1959–1960.

Plato, *The Dialogues of Plato.* 4th ed. Tr. by Benjamin Jowett. Oxford: Oxford University Press, 1953.

THE PYTHAGOREANS

And they say that he (Pythagoras) was once passing by when a dog was being beaten, and, filled with compassion, spoke these words, "Stop your beating, since I am sure it is the soul of a man dear to me which I recognized when I heard it cry out." *Xenophanes* (frag. 7)

Thus he (Pherecydes), who excelled in manliness and also in reverence, although dead, has a joyful existence for his soul—if indeed Pythagoras, wise beyond all men, had true insight and knew the matter thoroughly. *Ion of Chios* (frag. 4)

Both the ancients who concerned themselves with the gods, and the prophets as well, testify that the soul is yoked to the body on account of certain penalties, and is buried in it just as in a tomb. *Philolaus* (frag. 14)

Through Number, the soul is joined to the body and the immortal and likewise incorporeal Harmony . . . The body is loved by the soul, for without it it cannot use the senses. When, by death, the soul has been separated from the body, it lives an incorporeal existence in the world. *Philolaus* (spurious frag. 22)

HERACLITUS

When they are born they wish to live and to experience their fate—or, rather, they wish to rest, and they leave children behind to become their fate. (frag. 20)

Death is everything we see when we are awake, but everything we see when asleep—is sleep. (frag. 21)

There awaits men when they die what they neither hope for nor expect. (frag. 27)

It is death for souls to become water, and it is death for water to become earth; water comes into existence from the earth, and soul from water. (frag. 36)

Immortal mortals, mortal immortals: one lives the death of the other, one dies the life of the other. (frag. 62)

When he is there they rise up and become alert guards of the living and of the dead. (frag. 63)

It is joy—or death—for souls to become wet . . . We live their (the souls') death and they (the souls) live our death. (frag. 77)

They are the same thing within: living and dying, waking up and falling asleep, young and old. For the latter change into the former and the former change back into the latter. (frag. 88)

Corpses are more fit to be thrown out than dung. (frag. 96)

Souls down in Hades have a sense of smell. (frag. 98)

Souls of men killed in battle are purer than those who die of illness. (frag. 136)

EMPEDOCLES

And I will tell you something else: of all mortal things not one has birth, and there is no end of destructive death, but there is only a mixing and a changing of the mixed, and birth is a name among men. (frag. 8)

When the Elements have been mixed so as to form a man or a species of wild animals or of shrubs or of birds, and come into the light, then people say that there was a coming into being, and when the Elements separate, they call this in turn bad luck; they don't call it what is proper, and even I speak according to custom. (frag. 9)

Death the Avenger. (frag. 10)

Fools, since they do not have far-reaching thoughts, they who think that what does not exist before comes into being or that anything dies and perishes completely. (frag. 11)

But I will go back to that path of song which I formerly laid down, drawing off one stream of speech from another. When Strife arrived at the lowest depth of the vortex, and Love is in the middle of the whirl, in it all these things come together to be only one—not suddenly, but each joining together willingly, one from one place, one from another. And as these were mingled, innumerable kinds of mortal things were poured forth; but many unmixed things remain alternately with the mixed, all that Strife still aloft held in check, because it had not completely withdrawn from them, faultlessly, to the farthest boundaries of the circle, but parts of limbs remained within while other parts were passing out. And just as much as it continuously ran forth, so much did the gentle blameless immortal onset of Love continuously make its way. And immediately those things that had before learned to be immortal became mortal, and the formerly unmixed became mixed, changing paths. And as these were mingled, innumerable kinds of mortal things were poured forth, fitted with every kind of shape, a wonder to see. (frag. 35)

There exists an oracle of Necessity, an ancient decree of the gods, everlasting, secured by broad oaths: whenever anyone of the divinities who has obtained the lot of long life defiles his hands with the offense of murder, and Strife errs by swearing a false oath, for thirty thousand seasons he wanders apart from the blessed ones, undergoing birth through time in every kind of mortal shape, taking in turn the grievous paths of life. The power of air pursues him to the sea, the sea spits him up onto the dirt of the earth, the earth into the rays of the radiant sun, and the sun throws him into the vortex of the air. One takes him from the other, and all hate him. Even I am now one of these, a fugitive from the gods and a wanderer, one who trusted insane Strife. (frag. 115)

I have already been, once, a boy and a girl and a shrub and a bird and a silent fish of the sea. (frag. 117)

Strange and wretched race of mortals, completely luckless, you who are born amidst such struggles and groans. (frag. 124)

From living beings he made dead ones, exchanging their forms, (and from dead ones living). (frag. 125)

DEMOCRITUS

(To live badly) is not to live badly, but to die over a long period of time. (frag. 160)

The best thing for a man is to live his life as cheerfully as he can and with as little grief as possible. This would be the case if one did not look for pleasure in mortal things. (frag. 189)

Fools, they behave as if they hated living, but wish to live because of fear of Hades. (frag. 199)

Fleeing death, men pursue it. (frag. 203)

Fools, they reach out to life, fearing death. (frag. 205)

Fools, fearing death, they wish to grow old. (frag. 206)

It is necessary to understand that human life is feeble and of brief duration and mixed with many disasters and difficulties, in order that one may concern oneself with moderate possessions, and that hardship be measured against one's needs. (frag. 285)

The old man was young, but it is unclear whether the young man will reach old age; the accomplished good, therefore, is better than a still uncertain future. (frag. 295)

An old age perfect in all aspects is a mutilation: it possesses everything, and it is lacking in everything. (frag. 296)

Some men, not understanding the dissolution of mortal nature, and because of their awareness of the problems inherent in living, wear out the period of their lives in confusion and fear, making up false stories about the time after the final end. (frag. 297)

PLATO

The Apology

For the fear of death is indeed the pretence of wisdom, and not real wisdom, being a pretence of knowing the unknown; and no one knows whether death, of which men are afraid because they apprehend it to be the greatest evil, may not be the greatest good. Is not this ignorance of a disgraceful sort, the ignorance which is the conceit that a man knows what he does not know? And in this respect only I believe myself to differ from men in general, and may perhaps claim to be wiser than they are:—that whereas I know but little of the world below, I do not suppose that I know: but I do know that injustice and disobedience to a better, whether God or man, is evil and dishonourable, and I will never fear or avoid a possible good rather than a certain evil. (29a-b)

Let us reflect in another way, and we shall see that there is great reason to hope that death is a good; for one of two things—either death is a state of nothingness and utter unconsciousness, or, as men say, there is a change and migration of the soul from this world to another. Now if you suppose that there is no consciousness, but a sleep like the sleep of him who is undisturbed even by dreams, death will be an unspeakable gain. For if a person were to select the night in which his sleep was undisturbed even by dreams, and were to compare with this the other days and nights of his life, and then were to tell us how many days and nights he had passed in the course of his life better and more pleasantly than this one, I think that any man, I will not say a private man, but even the great king will not find many such days or nights, when compared with the others. Now if death be of such a nature, I say that to die is gain; for eternity is then only a single night. But if death is the journey to another place, and there, as men say, all the dead abide, what good, O my friends and judges, can be greater than this? If indeed when the pilgrim arrives in the world below, he is delivered from our earthly professors of justice, and finds the true judges who are said to give judgement there, Minos and Rhadamanthus and Aeacus and Tripto-lemus, and other sons of God who were righteous in their own life, that pilgrimage will be worth making. What would not a man give if he might converse with Orpheus and Musaeus and Hesiod and Homer? Nay, if this be true, let me die again and again. I myself, too, shall find a wonderful interest in there meeting and conversing with Palamedes, and Ajax the son of Telamon, and any other ancient hero who has suffered death through an unjust judgement; and there will be no small pleasure, as I think, in comparing my own experience with theirs. Above all, I shall then be able to continue my search into true and false knowledge, as in this world, so also in the next; and I shall find out who is wise, and who pretends to be wise, and is not. What would not a man give, O judges, to be able to examine the leader of the great Trojan expedition; or Odysseus or Sisyphus, or numberless others, men and women too! What infinite delight would there be in conversing with them and asking them questions! In another world they do not put a man to death for asking questions: assuredly not. For besides being happier than we are, they will be immortal, if what is said is true.

Wherefore, O judges, be of good cheer about death, and know of a certainty that no evil can happen to a good man, either in life or after death, and that he and his are not neglected by the gods. Nor has my own approaching end happened by mere chance; I see clearly that the time had arrived when it was better for me to die and be released from trouble; therefore the oracle gave no sign, and therefore also I am not at all angry with my condemners, or with my accusers. But although they have done me no harm, they intended it; and for this I may properly blame them.

Still I have a favour to ask of them. When my sons are grown up, I would ask you, O my friends, to punish them; I would have you trouble them, as I have troubled you, if they seem to care about riches, or anything, more than about virtue; or if they pretend to be something when they are really nothing,—then reprove them, as I have reproved you, for not caring about that for which they ought to care, and thinking that they are something when they are really nothing. And if you do this, I shall have received justice at your hands, and so will my sons. The hour of departure has arrived, and we go our ways—I to die, and you to live. Which is better God only knows. (40c-42a)

The Phaedo

I desire to prove to you that the real philosopher has reason to be of good cheer when he is about to die, and that after death he may hope to obtain the greatest good in the other world. And how this may be, Simmias and Cebes, I will endeavour to explain. For I deem that the true votary of philosophy is likely to be misunderstood by other men; they do not perceive that of his own accord he is always engaged in the pursuit of dying and death; and if this be so, and he has had the desire of death all his life long, why when his time comes should he repine at that which he has been always pursuing and desiring?

Simmias said laughingly: Though I am not altogether in a laughing humour, you have made me laugh, Socrates; for I cannot help thinking that the many when they hear your words will say how truly you have described philosophers, and our people at home will likewise say that philosophers are in reality moribund, and that they have found them out to be deserving of the death which they desire.

And they are right, Simmias, in thinking so, with the exception of the words 'they have found them out'; for they have not found out either in

what sense the true philosopher is moribund and deserves death, or
what manner of death he deserves. But enough of them:—let us discuss
the matter among ourselves. Do we attach a definite meaning to the
word 'death'?

To be sure, replied Simmias.

Is it not just the separation of soul and body? And to be dead is the
completion of this; when the soul exists by herself and is released from
the body, and the body is released from the soul. This, I presume, is
what is meant by death?

Just so, he replied.

There is another question, which will probably throw light on our
present inquiry if you and I can agree about it:—Ought the philosopher
to care about such pleasures—if they are to be called pleasures—as those
of eating and drinking?

Certainly not, answered Simmias.

And what about the pleasures of love—should he care for them?

By no means.

And will he think much of the other ways of indulging the body, for
example, the acquisition of costly raiment or sandals, or other adorn-
ments of the body? Instead of caring about them, does he not rather
despise anything more than nature needs? What do you say?

I should say that the true philosopher would despise them.

Would you not say that he is entirely concerned with the soul and not
with the body? He would like, as far as he can, to get away from the body
and to turn to the soul.

Quite true.

First, therefore, in matters of this sort philosophers, above all other
men, may be observed in every sort of way to dissever the soul from the
communion of the body.

Very true.

Whereas, Simmias, the rest of the world are of opinion that to him
who has no taste for bodily pleasures and no part in them, life is not
worth having; and that he who is indifferent about them is as good as
dead.

Perfectly true.

What again shall we say of the actual acquirement of knowledge?—is
the body, if invited to share in the inquiry, a hindrance or a help? I mean
to say, have sight and hearing, as found in man, any truth in them? Are
they not, as the poets are always repeating, inaccurate witnesses? and yet,
if even they are inaccurate and indistinct, what is to be said of the other
senses?—for you will allow that they are the best of them?

Certainly, he replied.

The when does the soul attain truth?—for in attempting to consider anything in company with the body she is obviously deceived by it.

True.

Then must not true reality be revealed to her in thought, if at all?

Yes.

And thought is best when the mind is gathered into herself and none of these things trouble her—neither sounds nor sights nor pain, nor again any pleasure,—when she takes leave of the body, and has as little as possible to do with it, when she has no bodily sense or desire, but is aspiring after true being?

Certainly.

And here again it is characteristic of the philosopher to despise the body; his soul runs away from his body and desires to be alone and by herself?

That is true.

Well, but there is another thing, Simmias: Is there or is there not an absolute justice?

Assuredly there is.

And an absolute beauty and absolute good?

Of course.

But did you ever behold any of them with your eyes?

Certainly not.

Or did you ever reach them with any other bodily sense?—and I speak not of these alone, but of absolute greatness, and health, and strength, and, in short, of the reality or true nature of everything. Is the truth of them ever perceived through the bodily organs? or rather, is not the nearest approach to the knowledge of their several natures made by him who so orders his intellectual vision as tc have the most exact conception of the essence of each thing which he considers?

Certainly.

And he attains to the purest knowledge of them who goes to each with the intellect alone, not introducing or intruding in the act of thought sight or any other sense together with reason, but with the intellect in its own purity searches into the truth of each thing in its purity; he who has got rid, as far as he can, of eyes and ears and, so to speak, of the whole body, these being in his opinion distracting elements which when they associate with the soul hinder her from acquiring truth and knowledge—who, if not he, is likely to attain to the knowledge of true being?

What you say has a wonderful truth in it, Socrates, replied Simmias.

And when real philosophers consider all these things, will they not be led to make a reflection which they will express in words something like the following? 'Have we not found', they will say, 'a path of thought

which seems to bring us and our argument to the conclusion, that while
we are in the body, and while the soul is mixed with the evils of the body,
our desire will not be satisfied? and our desire is of the truth. For the
body is a source of countless distractions by reason of the mere
requirement of food, and is liable also to diseases which overtake and
impede us in the pursuit of truth: it fills us full of loves, and lusts, and
fears, and fancies of all kinds, and endless foolery, and in very truth, as
men say, takes away from us the power of thinking at all. Whence come
wars, and fightings, and factions? whence but from the body and the
lusts of the body? All wars are occasioned by the love of money, and
money has to be acquired for the sake of the body and in slavish
ministration to it; and by reason of all these impediments we have no
time to give to philosophy; and, last and worst of all, even if the body
allows us leisure and we betake ourselves to some speculation, it is always
breaking in upon us, causing turmoil and confusion in our inquiries, and
so amazing us that we are prevented from seeing the truth. It has been
proved to us by experience that if we would have pure knowledge of
anything we must be quit of the body—the soul by herself must behold
things by themselves: and then we shall attain that which we desire, and
of which we say that we are lovers—wisdom; not while we live, but, as the
argument shows, only after death; for if while in company with the body
the soul cannot have pure knowledge, one of two things follows—either
knowledge is not to be attained at all, or, if at all, after death. For then,
and not till then, the soul will be parted from the body and exist by
herself alone. In this present life, we think that we make the nearest
approach to knowledge when we have the least possible intercourse or
communion with the body, and do not suffer the contagion of the bodily
nature, but keep ourselves pure until the hour when God himself is
pleased to release us. And thus getting rid of the foolishness of the body
we may expect to be pure and hold converse with the pure, and to know
of ourselves all that exists in perfection unalloyed, which, I take it, is no
other than the truth. For the impure are not permitted to lay hold of the
pure.' These are the sort of words, Simmias, which the true lovers of
knowledge cannot help saying to one another, and thinking. You would
agree; would you not?

Undoubtedly, Socrates.

But, O my friend, if this be true, there is great reason to hope that,
going whither I go, when I have come to the end of my journey I shall
fully attain that which has been the pursuit of our lives. And therefore
I accept with good hope this change of abode which is now enjoined
upon me, and not I only, but every other man who believes that his mind
has been made ready and that he is in a manner purified.

Certainly, replied Simmias.

And does it not follow that purification is nothing but that separation of the soul from the body, which has for some time been the subject of our argument; the habit of the soul gathering and collecting herself into herself from all sides out of the body; the dwelling in her own place alone, as in another life, so also in this, as far as she can;—the release of the soul from the chains of the body?

Very true, he said.

And this separation and release of the soul from the body is termed death?

To be sure, he said.

And the true philosophers, and they only, are ever seeking to release the soul. Is not the separation and release of the soul from the body their especial study?

That is true.

And, as I was saying at first, there would be a ridiculous contradiction in men studying to live as nearly as they can in a state like that of death, and yet repining when death comes upon them.

Clearly.

In fact, the true philosophers, Simmias, are always occupied in the practice of dying, wherefore also to them least of all men is death terrible. Look at the matter thus:—if they have been in every way estranged from the body, and are wanting to be alone with the soul, when this desire of theirs is being granted, how inconsistent would they be if they trembled and repined, instead of rejoicing at their departure to that place where, when they arrive, they hope to gain that which in life they desired—and their desire was for wisdom—and at the same time to be rid of the company of their enemy. Many a man who has lost by death an earthly love, or wife, or son, has been willing to go in quest of them to the world below, animated by the hope of seeing them there and of being with those for whom he yearned. And will he who is a true lover of wisdom, and is strongly persuaded in like manner that only in the world below he can worthily enjoy her, still repine at death? Will he not depart with joy? Surely he will, O my friend, if he be a true philosopher. For he will have a firm conviction that there, and there only, he can find wisdom in her purity. And if this be true, he would be very absurd, as I was saying, if he were afraid of death.

He would indeed, replied Simmias.

And when you see a man who is repining at the approach of death, is not his reluctance a sufficient proof that after all he is not a lover of wisdom, but a lover of the body, and probably at the same time a lover of either money or power, or both?

Quite so, he replied.

And then, Simmias, is not the quality we term courage most characteristic of the philosopher?

Certainly.

There is temperance again—I mean the quality which the vulgar also call by that name, the calm disdain and control of the passions—is not temperance a virtue belonging to those only who disdain the body, and who pass their lives in philosophy?

Most assuredly.

For the courage and temperance of other men, if you care to consider them, are really a paradox.

How so?

Well, he said, you are aware that death is regarded by men in general as a great evil.

Very true, he said.

And do not courageous men face death because they are afraid of yet greater evils?

That is quite true.

Then all but the philosophers are courageous only from fear, and because they are afraid; and yet that a man should be courageous from fear, and because he is a coward, is surely a strange thing.

Very true.

And are not the self-restrained exactly in the same case? They are temperate because in a sense they are intemperate—which might seem to be impossible, but is nevertheless the sort of thing which happens with this fatuous temperance. For there are pleasures which they are afraid of losing; and in their desire to keep them, they abstain from some pleasures because they are overcome by others; and although to be conquered by pleasure is called by men intemperance, to them the conquest of pleasure consists in being conquered by pleasure. And that is what I mean by saying that, in a sense, they are made temperate through intemperance.

Such appears to be the case.

Yet perhaps the exchange of one fear or pleasure or pain for another fear or pleasure or pain, of the greater for the less as if they were coins, is not the right exchange by the standard of virtue. O my dear Simmias, is there not one true coin for which all these ought to be exchanged?— and that is wisdom; and only in company with this do we attain real courage or temperance or justice. In a word, is not all true virtue the companion of wisdom, no matter what fears or pleasures or other similar goods or evils may or may not attend her? But the virtue which is made up of these goods, when they are severed from wisdom and exchanged with one another, is perhaps a mere facade of virtue, a slavish quality, wholly false and unsound; the truth is far different—temperance and justice and courage are in reality a purging away of all these things, and wisdom herself may be a kind of baptism into that purity. The founders of the mysteries would appear to have had a real meaning, and were not devoid of sense when they intimated in a figure long ago that he who passes unsanctified and uninitiated into the world below will lie in a slough, but that he who arrives there after initiation and purification will dwell with the gods. For 'many', as they say in the mysteries, 'are the thyrsus-bearers, but few are the mystics',—meaning, as I interpret the words, 'the true philosophers'. In the number of whom, during my whole life, I have been seeking, according to my ability, to find a place;—whether I have sought in a right way or not, and whether we have succeeded, we shall know for certain in a little while, if God will, when we arrive in the other world—such is my belief. And therefore I answer that I am right, Simmias and Cebes, in not grieving or repining at parting from you and my masters in this world, for I believe that I shall equally find good masters and friends in another world. If now I succeed in convincing you by my defence better than I did the Athenian judges, it will be well. (63b-69e)

When Socrates had finished, Cebes began to speak: I agree, Socrates, in the greater part of what you say. But in what concerns the soul, men are apt to be incredulous; they fear that when she has left the body her place may be nowhere, and that on the very day of death she may perish and come to an end immediately on her release from the body, issuing forth like smoke or breath, dispersing and vanishing away into nothingness in her flight. If she could only be collected into herself after she has obtained release from the evils of which you were speaking, there would be much reason for the goodly hope, Socrates, that what you say is true. But surely it requires a great deal of persuasion and proof to show that when the man is dead his soul yet exists, and has any force or intelligence.

True, Cebes, said Socrates; and shall I suggest that we speculate a little together concerning the probabilities of these things?

For my part, said Cebes, I should greatly like to know your opinion about them.

I reckon, said Socrates, that no one who heard me now, not even if he were one of my old enemies, the comic poets, could accuse me of idle talking about matters in which I have no concern:—If you please, then, we will proceed with the inquiry.

Suppose we consider the question whether the souls of men after death are or are not in the world below. There comes into my mind an ancient doctrine which affirms that they are there after they leave our world, and returning hither, are born again from the dead. Now if it be true that the living come from the dead, then our souls must exist in the other world, for if not, how could they have been born again? And this would be conclusive, if it were established that the living are born from the dead and have no other origin; but if this is not so, then other arguments will have to be adduced.

Very true, replied Cebes.

Then let us consider the whole question, not in relation to man only, but in relation to animals generally, and to plants, and to everything of which there is generation, and the proof will be easier. Are not all things which have opposites generated out of their opposites? I mean such things as the beautiful and the ugly, the just and the unjust—and there are innumerable other cases. Let us consider therefore whether it is necessary that a thing should come to be from its own opposite, if it has one, and from no other source: for example, anything which becomes greater must become greater after being less?

True.

And that which becomes less must have been once greater and then have become less?

Yes.

And the weaker is generated from the stronger, and the swifter from the slower?

Very true.

And the worse is from the better, and the more just is from the more unjust?

Of course.

And is this true of all opposites? and are we convinced that all of them are generated out of opposites?

Yes.

And in this universal opposition of all things, are there not also two intermediate processes which are ever going on, from one to the other opposite, and back again; for example, where there is a greater and a less there is also the intermediate process of increase and diminution, and so a thing is said to increase or to diminish?

Yes, he said.

And there are many other processes, such as analysis and combination, cooling and heating, which equally involve a passage into and out of one another. And this necessarily holds of all opposites, even though not always expressed in words—they are really generated out of one another, and there is a passing or process from one to the other of them?

Very true, he replied.

Well, and is there not an opposite of being alive, as sleep is the opposite of being awake?

True, he said.

And what is it?

Being dead, he answered.

And these, if they are opposites, are generated the one from the other, and have their two intermediate processes also?

Of course.

Now, said Socrates, I will analyse one of the two pairs of opposites which I have mentioned to you, and also its intermediate processes, and you shall analyse the other to me. The two members of the first pair are sleep and waking. The state of sleep is opposed to the state of waking, and out of sleeping waking is generated, and out of waking, sleeping; and the process of generation is in the one case falling asleep, and in the other waking up. Do you agree?

I entirely agree.

Then, suppose that you analyse life and death to me in the same manner. Is not the state of death opposed to that of life?

Yes.

And they are generated one from the other?

Yes.

What is generated from the living?

The dead.

And what from the dead?

I can only say in answer—the living.

Then the living, whether things or persons, Cebes, are generated from the dead?

So it would seem, he replied.

Then the inference is that our souls exist in the world below?

It appears so.

And one of the two processes or generations is visible—for surely the act of dying is visible?

Surely, he said.

What then is to be the result? Shall we exclude the opposite process? and shall we suppose nature to be lame in this respect? Must we not rather assign to the act of dying some corresponding process of generation?

Certainly, he replied.

And what is that?

Return to life.

And return to life, if there be such a thing, is the birth of the dead into the number of the living?

Quite true.

Then here is a new way by which we arrive at the conclusion that the living come from the dead, just as the dead come from the living; and we agreed that this, if true, would be adequate proof that the souls of the dead must exist in some place out of which they come again.

Yes, Socrates, he said; the conclusion seems to flow necessarily out of our previous admissions.

And that these admissions were not wrong, Cebes, he said, may be shown, I think, as follows: If generation were in a straight line only, and there were no compensation or circle in nature, no turn or return of elements into their opposites, then you know that all things would at last have the same form and suffer the same fate, and there would be no more generation of them.

What do you mean? he said.

A simple thing enough, which I will illustrate by the case of sleep, he replied. You know that if there were no alternation of sleeping and waking, the tale of the sleeping Endymion would in the end have no point, because all other things would be asleep too, and he would not be distinguishable from the rest. Or if there were combination only, and no analysis of substances, then we should soon have the chaos of Anaxagoras where 'all things were together'. And in like manner, my dear Cebes, if all things which partook of life were to die, and after they were dead remained in the form of death, and did not come to life again, all would at last be dead, and nothing would be alive—what other result could there be? For if living things had some other origin, and living things died, must not all things at last be swallowed up in death?

There is no escape, Socrates, said Cebes; and to me your argument seems to be absolutely true.

Yes, he said, Cebes, it is and must be so, in my opinion, and we have not been deluded in making these admissions; but I am confident that there truly is such a thing as living again, and that the living spring from the dead, and that the souls of the dead are in existence. (69e-72e)

Simmias and Cebes, and you others, will depart at some time or other. Me already, as a tragic poet would say, the voice of fate calls. Soon I must drink the poison; and I think that I had better repair to the bath first, in order that the women may not have the trouble of washing my body after I am dead.

When he had done speaking, Crito said: And have you any commands for us, Socrates—anything to say about your children, or any other matter in which we can serve you?

Nothing particular, Crito, he replied: only, as I have always told you, take care of yourselves; that is a service which you may be ever rendering to me and mine and to yourselves, whether you promise to do so or not. But if you have no thought for yourselves, and care not to walk in the path of life which I have shown you, not now for the first time, then however much and however earnestly you may promise at the moment, it will be of no avail.

We will do our best, said Crito: And in what way shall we bury you?

In any way that you like; but you must first get hold of me, and take care that I do not run away from you. Then he turned to us, and added with a smile:—I cannot make Crito believe that I am the same Socrates who have been talking and conducting the argument; he fancies that I am the other Socrates whom he will soon see, a dead body—and indeed he asks, How shall he bury me? And though I have spoken many words in the endeavour to show that when I have drunk the poison I shall leave you and go to the joys of the blessed,—these words of mine, with which I was comforting you and myself, have had, as I perceive, no effect upon Crito. And therefore I want you to be surety for me to him now, as at the trial he was surety to the judges for me: but let the promise be of another sort; for he was surety for me to the judges that I would remain, and you must be my surety to him that I shall not remain, but go away and depart; and then he will suffer less at my death, and not be grieved when he sees my body being burned or buried. I would not have him sorrow at my hard lot, or say at the burial, Thus we lay out Socrates, or, Thus we follow him to the grave or bury him; for be well assured, my dear Crito, that false words are not only evil in themselves, but they infect the soul with evil. Be of good cheer then and say that you are burying my body only, and do with that whatever is usual, and what you think best.

When he had spoken these words, he arose and went into a chamber to bathe; Crito followed him and told us to wait. So we remained behind, talking and thinking of the subject of discourse, and also of the greatness of our loss; he was like a father of whom we were being bereaved, and we were about to pass the rest of our lives as orphans. When he had taken the bath his children were brought to him—(he had two young sons and an elder one); and the women of his family also came, and he talked to them and gave them a few directions in the presence of Crito; then he dismissed them and returned to us.

Now the hour of sunset was near, for a good deal of time had passed while he was within. When he came out, he sat down with us again after his bath, but not much was said. Soon the jailer, who was the servant of the Eleven, entered and stood by him, saying:—To you, Socrates, whom after your time here I know to be the noblest and gentlest and best of all who ever came to this place, I will not impute the angry feelings of other men, who rage and swear at me, when, in obedience to the authorities,

I bid them drink the poison—indeed, I am sure that you are not angry with me; for others, as you are aware, and not I, are to blame. And so fare you well, and try to bear lightly what must needs be—you know my errand. Then bursting into tears he turned and started on his way out.

Socrates looked up at him and said: I return your good wishes, and will do as you bid. Then turning to us, he said, How charming the man is: since I have been in prison he has always been coming to see me, and at times he would talk to me, and was as good to me as could be, and now see how generously he sorrows on my account. We must do as he says, Crito; and therefore let the cup be brought, if the poison is prepared: if not, let the attendant prepare some.

But, said Crito, the sun is still upon the hill-tops, and is not yet set. I know that many a one takes the draught quite a long time after the announcement has been made to him, when he has eaten and drunk to his satisfaction and enjoyed the society of his chosen friends; do not hurry—there is time enough.

Socrates said: Yes, Crito, and therein they of whom you speak act logically, for they think that they will be gainers by the delay; but I likewise act logically in not following their example, for I do not think that I should gain anything by drinking the poison a little later; I should only be ridiculous in my own eyes for sparing and saving a life which is already down to its dregs. Please then to do as I say, and not to refuse me.

Crito made a sign to the servant, who was standing by; and he went out, and having been absent for some time, returned with the jailer carrying the cup of poison. Socrates said: You, my good friend, who are experienced in these matters, shall give me directions how I am to proceed. The man answered: You have only to walk about until your legs are heavy, and then to lie down, and the poison will act. At the same time he handed the cup to Socrates, who in the easiest and gentlest manner, without the least fear or change of colour or feature, and looking at the man sideways with that droll glance of his, took the cup and said: What do you say about making a libation out of this cup to any god? May I, or not? The man answered: We only prepare, Socrates, just so much as we deem enough. I understand, he said: but a prayer to the gods I may and must offer, that they will prosper my journey from this to the other world—even so—and so be it according to my prayer. Then he held his breath and drank off the poison quite readily and cheerfully. And hitherto most of us had been fairly able to control our sorrow; but now when we saw him drinking, and saw too that he had finished the draught, we could no longer forbear, and in spite of myself my own tears were flowing fast; so that I covered my face and wept, not indeed for him, but at the thought of my own calamity in having to part from such a friend. Nor was I the first; for Crito, when he found himself unable to restrain his tears, had got up, and I followed; and at that moment, Apollodorus, who had been weeping all the time, burst out in a loud and passionate cry which broke us all down. Socrates alone retained his calmness: What is this strange outcry? he said. I sent away the women mainly in order that they might not misbehave in this fashion, for I have been told that a man should die in peace. Be quiet then, and bear yourselves with fortitude. When we heard his words we were ashamed, and refrained our tears; and he walked about until, as he said, his legs began to fail, and then he lay on his back, according to the directions, and the man who gave him the poison now and then looked at his feet and legs; and after a while he pressed his foot hard, and asked him if he could feel; and he said, No; and then his leg, and so upwards and upwards, and showed us that he was becoming cold and stiff. And he felt them himself, and said: When the poison reaches the heart, that will be the end. He was beginning to grow cold about the groin, when he uncovered his face, for he had covered himself up, and said—they were his last words—he said: Crito, I owe a cock to Aesculapius; will you remember to pay the debt? The debt shall be paid, said Crito; is there anything else? There was no answer to this question; but in a minute or two a movement was heard, and the attendant uncovered him; his eyes were set, and Crito closed his eyes and mouth.

Such was the end, Echecrates, of our friend; concerning whom we may truly say that of all the men of his time whom we have known, he was the wisest and justest and best. (115a-118a)

Gorgias

Soc. Listen, then, as story-tellers say, to a very pretty tale, which I dare say that you may be disposed to regard as only a fantasy, but which, as I believe, is a true tale; what I am going to say, I offer as the truth. Homer tells us how Zeus and Poseidon and Pluto divided the empire which they inherited from their father. Now in the days of Cronos there existed a law respecting the destiny of man, which has always been, and still continues to be in Heaven,—that he who has lived all his life in justice and holiness shall go, when he is dead, to the Islands of the Blessed, and dwell there in perfect happiness out of the reach of evil; but that he who has lived unjustly and impiously shall go to the prison-house of vengeance and punishment, which is called Tartarus. And in the time of Cronos, and even quite lately in the reign of Zeus, the judgement was given on the very day on which the men were to die; the judges were alive, and the men were alive; and the consequence was that the cases were erroneously decided. Then Pluto and the authorities from the Islands of the Blessed came to Zeus, and said that the souls found their way to the wrong places. Zeus said: 'I shall put a stop to this; erroneous decisions are given, because the persons before the tribunal have their clothes on, for they are alive; and there are many who, having evil souls, are apparelled in fair bodies, or encased in wealth or hereditary rank, and, when the day of judgement arrives, numerous witnesses come forward and testify on their behalf that they have lived righteously. The judges are awed by them, and they themselves too have their clothes on when judging; their eyes and ears and their whole bodies are interposed as a veil before their own souls. All this is a hindrance to them, both the clothes of the judges and the clothes of the judged.—In the first place, therefore, I will deprive men of the foreknowledge of death, which they possess at present; this power which they have Prometheus has already received my orders to take from them: in the second place, they shall all be entirely stripped before they are judged, for they shall be judged when they are dead; and the judge too shall be naked, that is to say, dead—he with his naked soul shall pierce into the other naked souls as they are after death without warning, deprived of all their kindred, and leaving their brave attire strewn upon the earth—conducted in this manner, the judgement will be just. I knew all about the matter before any of you, and therefore I have appointed sons of my own to be judges; two from Asia, Minos and Rhadamanthus, and one from Europe, Aeacus. And these, when they are dead, shall give judgement in the meadow at the parting of the ways, whence the two roads lead, one to the Islands of the Blessed, and the other to Tartarus. Rhadamanthus shall judge those who come from Asia, and Aeacus those who come from Europe. And to Minos I shall give the primacy, and he shall be a court of appeal, in case either of the two others are in any doubt:—then the judgement respecting the last journey of men will be as just as possible.'

From this tale, Callicles, which I have heard and believe, I draw the following inferences:—Death, if I am right, is in the first place the separation from one another of two things, soul and body; nothing else. And after they are separated each of them retains, with little change, the same condition as in life; the body keeps the same habit, and the results of treatment or accident are all distinctly visible in it: for example, he who by nature or training or both, was a tall man while he was alive, will remain as he was, after he is dead, and the fat man will remain fat, and so on; and the dead man, who in life had a fancy to have flowing hair, will have flowing hair. And if he was a worthless rogue, and bore on his body the marks of blows, scars from the whip or from other corporal punishments when he was alive, you might see the same in the dead body; and if his limbs were broken or misshapen when he was alive, the same appearance would be visible in the dead. And in a word, whatever was the habit of the body during life would be evident after death, either perfectly, or in a great measure and for a certain time. And I should imagine that this is equally true of the soul, Callicles; when the soul is stripped of the body, everything in it is laid open to view—all its natural features and all the characteristics it has acquired in each of its various activities. And when they come to the judge, as those from Asia come to Rhadamanthus, he stops them and inspects them one by one quite impartially, not knowing whose the soul is: often he may lay hands on the soul of some king or potentate such as the Great King, and discerns no soundness in him, but a soul marked with the whip, and full of the scars of perjuries and crimes with which each action has stained him, and all crooked with falsehood and imposture, and without straightness, because he has lived without truth. Him Rhadamanthus beholds, full of all the deformity and disproportion which is caused by licence and luxury and insolence and incontinence, and dispatches him ignominiously to his prison, and there he undergoes the punishment which he deserves.

Now the proper office of all punishment is twofold: he who is rightly punished ought either to become better and profit by it, or he ought to be made an example to his fellows, that they may see what he suffers, and fear to suffer the like, and become better. Those who are improved when they are punished by gods and men, are those whose sins are curable; and they are improved, as in this world so also in another, by pain and suffering; for there is no other way in which they can be delivered from their evil. But they who have been guilty of the worst crimes, and are incurable by reason of their crimes, are made examples; as they are incurable, they get no good themselves, but others get good when they behold them enduring for ever the most terrible and painful and fearful sufferings as the penalty of their sins—there they are, hanging up in the prison-house of the world below just as examples, a spectacle and a warning to all unrighteous men who come thither. And among them, as I confidently affirm, will be found Archelaus, if Polus truly reports of him, and any other tyrant who is like him. Of these fearful examples, most, as I believe, are taken from the class of tyrants and kings and potentates and public men, for they are the authors of the greatest and most impious crimes because they have the power. And Homer witnesses to the truth of this; for they are always kings and potentates whom he has described as suffering everlasting punishment in the world below: such were Tantalus and Sisyphus and Tityus. But no one ever described Thersites, or any private person who was a villain, as suffering everlasting punishment, or as incurable. For to commit the worst crimes, as I am inclined to think, was not in his power, and he was therefore happier than those who had the power. No, Callicles, the very bad men come from the class of those who have power. And yet in that very class there may arise good men, and worthy of all admiration they are when they do arise; for where there is great power to do wrong, to live and to die justly is a hard thing, and greatly to be praised, and few there are who attain to this. Such good and true men, however, there have been at Athens and in other states, and I think will be hereafter— men eminent in this virtue, the virtue of righteous fulfilment of their trust; and there is one who is quite famous all over Hellas, Aristeides, the son of Lysimachus. But, in general, great men are also bad, my friend.

As I was saying, Rhadamanthus, when he gets a soul of the bad kind, knows nothing about him, neither who he is, nor who his parents are; he knows only that he has got hold of a villain; and seeing this, he stamps him as curable or incurable, and sends him away to Tartarus, whither he goes and receives his proper recompense. Or, again, he looks with admiration on the soul of some just one who has lived in holiness and truth; he may have been a private man or not; and I should say, Callicles, that he is most likely to have been a philosopher who has done his own work, and not troubled himself with the doings of other men in his lifetime; him Rhadamanthus sends to the Islands of the Blessed. Aeacus does the same; and they both have sceptres, and judge; but Minos alone has a golden sceptre and sits there watching, as Odysseus in Homer declares that he saw him:

'Holding a sceptre of gold, and giving laws to the dead.'

Now I, Callicles, am persuaded of the truth of these things, and I consider how I shall present my soul whole and undefiled before the judge in that day. Renouncing the honours at which the world aims, I desire only to know the truth, and to live as well as I can, and, when I die, to die as well as I can. And, to the utmost of my power, I exhort all other men to do the same. And, in return for your exhortation of me, I exhort you also to enter upon this way of life, and to engage in this combat, which is, I maintain, greater than every other earthly conflict. And I retort your reproach of me, and say that you will not be able to defend yourself when the day of trial and judgement, of which I was speaking, comes upon you; you will go before the judge, the son of Aegina, and, when he has got you in his grip and is carrying you off, you will gape and your head will swim round, just as mine would in the courts of this world, and very likely some one will shamefully box you on the ears, and put upon you every sort of insult.

Perhaps this may appear to you to be only an old wife's tale, which you will contemn. And there might be reason in your contemning such tales, if by searching we could find out anything better or truer: but now you see that you and Polus and Gorgias, who are the three wisest of the Greeks of our day, are not able to show that we ought to live any life but this, which assuredly profits in the next world as well as here. And of all that has been said, nothing remains unshaken but the saying that to do injustice is more to be avoided than to suffer injustice, and that the reality and not the appearance of virtue is to be followed above all things, as well in public as in private life; and that when a man is doing wrong in any respect, he is to be chastised, because the next best thing to a man being just is that he should become just by correction and punishment; also that he should avoid all flattery of himself as well as of others, of the few or of the many: and rhetoric should be used by him, and all his actions should be done always, with a view to justice.

Follow me then, and I will lead you where you will be happy in life and after death, as the argument shows. And never mind if some one despises you as a fool, and insults you, if he has a mind; for heaven's sake, let him strike you, and do you be of good cheer, and do not mind the insulting blow, for you will never come to any harm in the practice of virtue if you are a really good and true man. When we have practised virtue together, we will apply ourselves to politics, if that seems desirable, or we will advise about whatever else may seem good to us, for we shall be better able to judge then. In our present condition, such as it clearly is, it would be disgraceful for us to give ourselves airs as though we were of some consequence, for even on the most important subjects we are always changing our minds; so utterly ignorant are we! Let us, then, take our recent argument as our guide, which has revealed to us that the best way of life is to practise justice and every virtue in life and death. This way let us go; and in this exhort all men to follow, not in the way to which you trust and in which you exhort me to follow you; for that way, Callicles, is nothing worth. (523a-527e)

The Republic

Well, I said, I will tell you a tale; not one of the tales which Odysseus tells to the hero Alcinous, yet this too is a tale of a hero, Er the son of Armenius, a Pamphylian by birth. He was slain in battle, and ten days afterwards, when the bodies of the dead were taken up already in a state of corruption, his body was found unaffected by decay, and carried away home to be buried. And on the twelfth day, as he was lying on the funeral pile, he returned to life and told them what he had seen in the other world. He said that when his soul left the body it went on a journey with a great company, and that they came to a mysterious place at which there were two openings in the earth; they were near together, and over against them were two other openings in the heaven above. In the intermediate space there were judges seated, who commanded the just, after they had given judgement on them and had bound their sentences in front of them, to ascend by the way up through the heaven on the right hand; and in like manner the unjust were bidden by them to descend by the lower way on the left hand; these also bore tokens of all their deeds, but fastened on their backs. He drew near, and they told him that he was to be the messenger who would carry the report of the other world to men, and they bade him hear and see all that was to be heard and seen in that place. Then he beheld and saw on one side the souls departing at either opening of heaven and earth when sentence had been given on them; and at the two other openings other souls, some ascending out of the earth dusty and worn with travel, some descending out of heaven clean and bright. And arriving ever and anon they seemed to have come from a long journey, and they went forth with gladness into the meadow, where they encamped as at a festival; and those who knew one another embraced and conversed, the souls which came from earth curiously inquiring about the things above, and the souls which came from heaven about the things beneath. And they told one another of what had happened by the way, those from below weeping and sorrowing at the remembrance of the things which they had endured and seen in their journey beneath the earth (now the journey lasted a thousand years), while those from above were describing heavenly delights and visions of inconceivable beauty. The full story, Glaucon, would take too long to tell; but the sum was this:—He said that for every wrong which they had done and every person whom they had injured they had suffered tenfold; or once in a hundred years—such being reckoned to be the length of man's life, and the penalty being thus paid ten times in a thousand years. If, for example, there were any who had been the cause of many deaths by the betrayal of cities or armies, or had cast many into slavery, or been accessory to any other ill treatment, for all their offences, and on behalf of each man wronged, they were afflicted with tenfold pain, and the rewards of beneficence and justice and holiness were in the same proportion. I need hardly repeat what he said concerning young children dying almost as soon as they were born. Of piety and impiety to gods and parents, and of murder, there were retributions other and greater far which he described. He mentioned that he was present when one of the spirits asked another, 'Where is Ardiaeus the Great?' (Now this Ardiaeus lived a thousand years before the time of Er: he had been the tyrant of some city of Pamphylia and had murdered his aged father and his elder brother, and was said to have committed many other abominable crimes.) The answer of the other spirit was: 'He comes not hither and will never come. And this', said he, 'was one of the dreadful sights which we ourselves witnessed. We were at the mouth of the cavern, and, having completed all our experiences, were about to reascend, when of a sudden, we saw Ardiaeus and several others, most of whom were tyrants; but there were also some private individuals who had been great criminals: they were just, as they fancied, about to return into the upper world, but the mouth, instead of admitting them, gave a roar, whenever any of these whose wickedness was incurable or who had not been sufficiently punished tried to ascend; and then wild men of fiery aspect, who were standing by and heard the sound, seized and carried them off; but Ardiaeus and others they bound head and foot and hand, and threw them down, and flayed them with scourges, and dragged them along the road outside the entrance, carding them on thorns like wool, and declaring to the passers-by what were their crimes, and that they were being taken away to be cast into Tartarus.' And of all the many terrors of every kind which they had endured, he said that there was none like the terror which each of them felt at that moment, lest they should hear the voice; and when there was silence, one by one they ascended with exceeding joy. These, said Er, were the penalties and retributions, and there were blessings as great.

Now when each band which was in the meadow had tarried seven days, on the eighth they were obliged to proceed on their journey, and, on the fourth day after, he said that they came to a place where they could see from above a line of light, straight as a column, extending right through the whole heaven and through the earth, in colour resembling the rainbow, only brighter and purer; another day's journey brought them to the place, and there, in the midst of the light, they saw the ends of the chains of heaven let down from above: for this light is the belt of heaven, and holds together the circumference of the universe, like the under-girders of a trireme. From these ends is extended the spindle of Necessity, on which all the revolutions turn. The shaft and hook of this spindle are made of adamant, and the whorl is made partly of steel and also partly of other materials. The nature of the whorl is as follows; it is, in outward shape, like the whorl used on earth; and his description of it implied that there is one large hollow whorl which is quite scooped out, and into this is fitted another lesser one, and another, and another, and four others, making eight in all, like vessels which fit into one another;

the whorls show their circular edges on the upper side, and on their lower side all together form one continuous whorl. This is pierced by the shaft which is driven home through the centre of the eighth. The first and outermost whorl has the rim broadest, and the seven inner whorls are narrower, in the following proportions—the sixth is next to the first in size, the fourth next to the sixth; then comes the eighth; the seventh is fifth, the fifth is sixth, the third is seventh, last and eighth comes the second. The largest [or fixed stars] is spangled, and the seventh [or sun] is brightest; the eighth [or moon] coloured by the reflected light of the seventh; the second and fifth [Saturn and Mercury] are in colour like one another, and yellower than the preceding; the third [Venus] has the whitest light; the fourth [Mars] is reddish; the sixth [Jupiter] is in whiteness second. Now the whole spindle has the same motion; but, as the whole revolves in one direction, the seven inner circles move slowly in the other, and of these the swiftest is the eighth; next in swiftness are the seventh, sixth, and fifth, which move together; third in swiftness appeared to move, because of this contrary motion, the fourth; the third appeared fourth and the second fifth. The spindle turns on the knees of Necessity; and on the upper surface of each circle stands a siren, who goes round with them, chanting a single tone or note. The eight together form one harmony; and round about, at equal intervals, there is another band, three in number, each sitting upon her throne: these are the Fates, daughters of Necessity, who are clothed in white robes and have chaplets upon their heads, Lachesis and Clotho and Atropos, who accompany with their voices the harmony of the sirens—Lachesis singing of the past, Clotho of the present, Atropos of the future; Clotho from time to time assisting with a touch of her right hand the revolution of the outer circle of the whorl or spindle, and Atropos with her left hand touching and guiding the inner ones, and Lachesis laying hold of either in turn, first with one hand and then with the other.

When Er and the spirits arrived, their duty was to go at once to Lachesis; but first of all there came a prophet who arranged them in order; then he took from the knees of Lachesis lots and samples of lives, and having mounted a high pulpit, spoke as follows: 'Hear the word of Lachesis, the daughter of Necessity. Mortal souls, behold a new cycle of life and mortality. Your genius will not be allotted to you, but you will choose your genius; and let him who draws the first lot have the first choice, and the life which he chooses shall be his destiny. Virtue is free, and as a man honours or dishonours her he will have more or less of her; the responsibility is with the chooser—God is not responsible.' When the Interpreter had thus spoken he scattered lots indifferently among them all, and each of them took up the lot which fell near him, all but Er himself (he was not allowed), and each as he took his lot perceived the number which he had obtained. Then the Interpreter placed on the ground before them the patterns of lives; and there were many more lives than the souls present, and they were of all sorts. There were lives of every animal and of man in every condition. And there were tyrannies among them, some lasting out the tryant's life, others which broke off in the middle and came to an end in poverty and exile and beggary; and there were lives of famous men, some who were famous for their form and beauty as well as for their strength and success in games, or, again, for their birth and the qualities of their ancestors; and some who were the reverse of famous for the opposite qualities. And of women likewise. The disposition of the soul was not, however, included in them, because the soul, when choosing a new life, must of necessity become different. But there was every other quality, and they all mingled with one another, and also with elements of wealth and poverty, and disease and health; and there were also states intermediate in these respects.

And here, my dear Glaucon, is the supreme peril of our human state; and therefore each one of us must take the utmost care to forsake every other kind of knowledge and seek and study one thing only, if peradventure he may be able to discover someone who will make him able to discern between a good and an evil life, and so to choose always and everywhere the better life as he has opportunity. He should consider the bearing of all these things which have been mentioned severally and collectively upon the excellence of a life; he should know what the effect of beauty is, for good or evil, when combined with poverty or wealth in this or that kind of soul, and what are the good and evil consequences of noble and humble birth, of private and public station, of strength and weakness, of cleverness and dullness, and of all the natural and acquired gifts of the soul, and the operation of them when blended with one another; he will then look at the nature of the soul, and from the consideration of all these qualities he will be able to determine which is the better and which is the worse; and so he will choose, giving the name of evil to the life which will tend to make his soul more unjust, and good to the life which will make his soul more just; all else he will disregard. For we have seen and know that this is the best choice both in life and after death. A man must take with him into the world below an adamantine faith in truth and right, that there too he may be undazzled by the desire of wealth or the other allurements of evil, lest he be drawn into tyrannies and similar activities, and do irremediable wrongs to others and suffer yet worse himself; but may know how to choose a life moderate in these respects and avoid the extremes on either side, as far as possible, not only in this life but in all that which is to come. For this way brings men to their greatest happiness.

And according to the report of the messenger from the other world this was what the prophet said at the time: 'Even for the last comer, if he chooses wisely and will live diligently, there is appointed a happy and not undesirable existence. Let not him who chooses first be careless, and let not the last despair.' And when he had spoken, he who had the first choice came forward and in a moment chose the greatest tyranny; his mind having been darkened by folly and sensuality, he had not made any thorough inspection before he chose, and did not perceive that he was fated, among other evils, to devour his own children. But when he had time to examine the lot and saw what was in it, he began to beat his breast and lament over his choice, forgetting the proclamation of the prophet; for, instead of throwing the blame of his misfortune on himself, he accused chance and the gods, and everything rather than himself. Now he was one of those who came from heaven, and in a former life had dwelt in a well-ordered State, virtuous from habit only, and without philosophy. And for the most part it was true of others who were caught in this way, that the greater number of them came from heaven and therefore they had never been schooled by trial, whereas the pilgrims who came from earth having themselves suffered and seen others suffer were not in a hurry to choose. And owing to this inexperience of theirs, and also to the accident of the lot, the majority of the souls exchanged a good destiny for an evil or an evil for a good. For if a man had always on his arrival in this world dedicated himself from the first to sound philosophy, and had been moderately fortunate in the number of the lot, he might, as the messenger reported, be happy here, and also his journey to another life and return to this, instead of being rough and underground, would be smooth and heavenly. Most curious, he said, was the spectacle—sad and laughable and strange; for the choice of the souls was in most cases based on their experience of a previous life. There he saw the soul which had once been Orpheus choosing the life of a swan out of enmity to the race of women, hating to be born of a woman because they had been his murderers; he beheld also the soul of Thamyras choosing the life of a nightingale; birds, on the other hand, like the swan and other musicians, wanting to be men. The soul which obtained the twentieth lot chose the life of a lion, and this was the soul of Ajax the son of Telamon, who would not be a man, remembering the injustice which was done him in the judgement about the arms. The next was Agamemnon, who took the life of an eagle, because, like Ajax, he hated human nature by reason of his sufferings. About the middle came the lot of Atalanta; she, seeing the great fame of an athlete, was unable to resist the temptation: and after her there followed the soul of Epeus the son of Panopeus passing into the nature of a woman skilled in some craft; and far away among the last who chose, the soul of the jester Thersites was putting on the form of a monkey. There came also the soul of Odysseus having yet to make a choice, and his lot happened to be the last of them all. Now the recollection of former toils had disenchanted him of ambition, and he went about for a considerable time in search of the life of a private man who had no cares; he had some difficulty in finding this, which was lying about and had been neglected by everybody else; and when he saw it, he said that he would have done the same had his lot been first instead of last, and gladly chose it. And not only did men pass into animals, but I must also mention that there were animals tame and wild who changed into one another and into corresponding human natures—the righteous into the gentle and the unrighteous into the savage, in all sorts of combinations.

All the souls had now chosen their lives, and they went in the order of their choice to Lachesis, who sent with them the genius whom they had severally chosen, to be the guardian of their lives and the fulfiller of the choice: this genius led the souls first to Clotho, and drew them within the revolution of the spindle impelled by her hand, thus ratifying the destiny of each; and then, when they were fastened to this, carried them to Atropos, who spun the threads and made them irreversible, whence without turning round they passed beneath the throne of Necessity; and when they had all passed, they marched on to the plain of Forgetfulness, in intolerable scorching heat, for the plain was a barren waste destitute of trees and verdure; and then towards evening they encamped by the river of Unmindfulness, whose water no vessel can hold; of this they were all obliged to drink a certain quantity, and those who were not saved by wisdom drank more than was necessary; and each one as he drank forgot all things. Now after they had gone to rest, about the middle of the night there was a thunderstorm and earthquake, and then in an instant they were driven upwards in all manner of ways to their birth, like stars shooting. He himself was hindered from drinking the water. But in what manner or by what means he returned to the body he could not say; only in the morning, awaking suddenly, he found himself lying on the pyre.

And thus, Glaucon, the tale has been saved and has not perished, and will save us if we are obedient to the word spoken; and we shall pass safely over the river of Forgetfulness and our soul will not be defiled. Wherefore my counsel is that we hold fast ever to the heavenly way and follow after justice and virtue always, considering that the soul is immortal and able to endure every sort of good and every sort of evil.

Thus shall we live dear to one another and to the gods, both while remaining here and when, like conquerors in the games who go round to gather gifts, we receive our reward. And it shall be well with us both in this life and in the pilgrimage of a thousand years which we have been describing. (614b-621d)

Phaedrus

But first of all, let us view the affections and actions of the soul divine and human, and try to ascertain the truth about them. The beginning of our proof is as follows:—

The soul through all her being is immortal, for that which is ever in motion is immortal; but that which moves another and is moved by another, in ceasing to move ceases also to live. Only the self-moving, since it cannot depart from itself, never ceases to move, and is the fountain and beginning of motion to all that moves besides. Now, the beginning is unbegotten, for that which is begotten must have a beginning; but this itself cannot be begotten of anything, for if it were dependent upon something, then the begotten would not come from a *beginning*. But since it is unbegotten, it must also be indestructible. For surely if a beginning were destroyed, then it could neither come into being itself from any source, nor serve as the beginning of other things, if it be true that all things must have a beginning. Thus it is proved that the self-moving is the beginning of motion; and this can neither be destroyed nor begotten, else the whole heavens and all creation would collapse and stand still, and, lacking all power of motion, never again have birth. But whereas the self-moving is proved to be immortal, he who affirms that this is the very meaning and essence of the soul will not be put to confusion. For every body which is moved from without is soul-less, but that which is self-moved from within is animate, and our usage makes it plain what is the nature of the soul. But if this be true, that the soul is identical with the self-moving, it must follow of necessity that the soul is unbegotten and immortal. Enough of her immortality: let up pass to the description of her form.

To show her true nature would be a theme of large and more than mortal discourse, but an image of it may be given in a briefer discourse within the scope of man; in this way, then, let us speak. Let the soul be compared to a pair of winged horses and charioteer joined in natural union. Now the horses and the charioteers of the gods are all of them noble and of noble descent, but those of other races are mixed. First, you must know that the human charioteer drives a pair; and next, that one of his horses is noble and of noble breed, and the other is ignoble and of ignoble breed; so that the management of the human chariot cannot but be a difficult and anxious task. I will endeavour to explain to you in what way the mortal differs from the immortal creature. The soul in her totality has the care of inanimate being everywhere, and traverses the whole heaven in divers forms appearing;—when perfect and fully winged she soars upward, and orders the whole world; whereas the imperfect soul, losing her wings and drooping in her flight at last settles on the solid ground—there, finding a home, she receives an earthly frame which appears to be self-moved, but is really moved by her power; and this composition of soul and body is called a living and mortal creature. For immortal no such union can be reasonably believed to be; although fancy, not having seen nor surely known the nature of God, may imagine an immortal creature having both a body and also a soul which are united throughout all time. Let that, however, be as God wills, and be spoken of acceptably to him. And now let us ask the reason why the soul loses her wings!

The wing is the corporeal element which is most akin to the divine, and which by nature tends to soar aloft and carry that which gravitates downwards into the upper region, which is the habitation of the gods. The divine is beauty, wisdom, goodness, and the like; and by these the wing of the soul is nourished, and grows apace; but when fed upon evil and foulness and the opposite of good, wastes and falls away. Zeus, the mighty lord, holding the reins of a winged chariot, leads the way in heaven, ordering all and taking care of all; and there follows him the array of gods and demi-gods, marshalled in eleven bands; Hestia alone abides at home in the house of heaven; of the rest they who are reckoned among the princely twelve march in their appointed order. They see many blessed sights in the inner heaven, and there are many ways to and fro, along which the blessed gods are passing, every one doing his own work; he may follow who will and can, for jealousy has no place in the celestial choir. But when they go to banquet and festival, then they move up the steep to the top of the vault of heaven. The chariots of the gods in even poise, obeying the rein, glide rapidly; but the others labour, for the vicious steed goes heavily, weighing down the charioteer to the earth when his steed has not been thoroughly trained:—and this is the hour of agony and extremest conflict for the soul. For the immortals, when they are at the end of their course, go forth and stand upon the outside of heaven; its revolution carries them round, and they behold the things beyond. But of the heaven which is above the heavens, what earthly poet ever did or ever will sing worthily? It is such as I will describe; for I must dare to speak the truth, when truth is my theme. There abides the very being with which true knowledge is concerned; the colourless, formless, intangible essence, visible only to mind, the pilot of the soul. The divine intelligence, being nurtured upon mind and pure knowledge, and the intelligence of every soul which is capable of receiving the food proper to it, rejoices at beholding reality once more, after so long a time, and gazing upon truth, is replenished and made glad, until the revolution of the world brings her round again to the same place. In the revolution she beholds justice, and temperance, and knowledge absolute, not that to which becoming belongs, nor that which is found, in varying forms, in one or other of those regions which we men call *real,* but real knowledge really present where true being is. And beholding the other true existences in like manner, and feasting upon them, she passes down into the interior of the heavens and returns home; and there the charioteer putting up his horses at the stall, gives them ambrosia to eat and nectar to drink.

Such is the life of the gods; but of other souls, that which follows God best and is likest to him lifts the head of the charioteer into the outer world, and is carried round in the revolution, troubled indeed by the steeds, and with difficulty beholding true being; while another only rises and falls, and sees, and again fails to see by reason of the unruliness of the steeds. The rest of the souls are also longing after the upper world and they all follow, but not being strong enough they are carried round below the surface, plunging, treading on one another, each striving to be first; and there is confusion and perspiration and the extremity of effort; and many of them are lamed or have their wings broken through the ill driving of the charioteers; and all of them after a fruitless toil, not having attained to the mysteries of true being, go away, and feed upon opinion [or appearance]. The reason why the souls exhibit this exceeding eagerness to behold the Plain of Truth is that pasturage is found there, which is suited to the highest part of the soul; and the wing on which the soul soars is nourished with this. And there is a law of Destiny, that the soul which attains any vision of truth in company with a god is preserved from harm until the next period, and if attaining always is always unharmed. But when she is unable to follow, and fails to behold the truth, and through some ill-hap sinks beneath the double load of forgetfulness and vice, and her wings fall from her and she drops to the ground, then the law ordains that this soul shall at her first birth pass, not into any other animal, but only into man; and the soul which has seen most of truth shall be placed in the seed from which a philosopher, or artist, or some musical and loving nature will spring; that which has seen truth in the second degree shall be some righteous king or warrior chief; the soul which is of the third class shall be a politician, or economist, or trader; the fourth shall be a lover of gymnastic toils, or a physician; the fifth shall lead the life of a prophet or hierophant; to the sixth the character of a poet or some other imitative artist will be assigned; to the seventh the life of an artisan or husbandman; to the eighth that of a sophist or demagogue; to the ninth that of a tyrant;—all these are states of probation, in which he who does righteously improves, and he who does unrighteously deteriorates, his lot.

Ten thousand years must elapse before the soul of each one can return to the place from whence she came, for she cannot grow her wings in less, save only the soul of a philosopher, guileless and true, or of a lover, who has been guided by philosophy. And these when the third period comes round, if they have chosen this life three times in succession, have wings given them, and go away at the end of three thousand years. But the others receive judgement when they have completed their first life, and after the judgement they go, some of them to the houses of correction which are under the earth, and are punished; others to some place in heaven whither they are lightly borne by justice, and there they live in a manner worthy of the life which they led here when in the form of men. And in the thousandth year, both arrive at a place where they must draw lots and choose their second life, and they may take any which they please. And now the soul of a man may pass into the life of a beast, or that which has once been a man return again from the beast into human form. But the soul which has never seen the truth will not pass into the human form. For a man must have intelligence by what is called the Idea, a unity gathered together by reason from the many particulars of sense. This is the recollection of those things which our soul once saw while following God—when regardless of that which we now call being she raised her head up towards the true being. And therefore the mind of the philosopher alone has wings; and this is just, for he is always, according to the measure of his abilities, clinging in recollection to those things in which God abides, and in beholding which He is what He is. And he who employs aright these memories is ever being initiated into perfect mysteries and alone becomes truly perfect. But, as he forgets earthly interests and is rapt in the divine, the vulgar deem him mad, and rebuke him; they do not see that he is inspired.

Thus far I have been speaking of the fourth and last kind of madness, which is imputed to him who, when he sees the beauty of earth, is transported with the recollection of the true beauty; he would like to fly away, but he cannot; he is like a bird fluttering and looking upward and careless of the world below; and he is therefore thought to be mad. And I have shown this of all inspirations to be the noblest and highest and the offspring of the highest to him who has or shares in it, and that he who loves the beautiful is called a lover because he partakes of it. For, as has been already said, every soul of man has in the way of nature beheld true being; this was the condition of her passing into the form of man. But all souls do not easily recall the things of the other world; they may have seen them for a short time only, or they may have been unfortunate in their earthly lot, and, having had their hearts turned to unrighteousness through some corrupting influence, they may have lost the memory of the holy things which once they saw. Few only retain an adequate remembrance of them; and they, when they behold here any image of that other world, are rapt in amazement; but they are ignorant of what this rapture means, because they do not clearly perceive. For there is no radiance in our earthly copies of justice or temperance or those other things which are precious to souls: they are seen through a glass dimly; and there are few who, going to the images, behold in them the realities, and these only with difficulty. But beauty could be seen, brightly shining, by all who were with that happy band,—we philosophers following in the train of Zeus, others in company with other gods; at which time we beheld the beatific vision and were initiated into a mystery which may be truly called most blessed, celebrated by us in our state of innocence, before we had any experience of evils to come, when we were admitted to the sight of apparitions innocent and simple and calm and happy, which we beheld shining in pure light, pure ourselves and not yet enshrined in that living tomb which we carry about, now that we are imprisoned in the body, like an oyster in his shell. (245c-250c)

Meno

Soc. I have heard from certain men and women skilled in things divine that—

Men. What did they say?

Soc. They spoke of a glorious truth, as I conceive.

Men. What is it? and who are they?

Soc. Some of them are priests and priestesses, who have striven to learn how to give a reasonable account of the things with which they concern themselves: there are poets also, like Pindar, and the many others who are inspired. And they say—mark, now, and see whether their words are true—they say that the soul of man is immortal, and at one time has an end, which is termed dying, and at another time is born again, but is never destroyed. And the moral is, that a man ought to live always in perfect holiness. *'For in the ninth year Persephone sends the souls of those from whom she has received the penalty of ancient crime back again from beneath into the light of the sun above, and these are they who become noble kings and mighty men and great in wisdom and are for ever called saintly heroes.'* The soul, then, as being immortal and having been born again many times, and having seen all things that exist, whether in this world or in the world below, has knowledge of them all; and it is no wonder that she should be able to call to remembrance all that she ever knew about virtue, and about everything; for as all nature is akin, and the soul has learned all things, there is no difficulty in a man eliciting out of a single recollection all the rest—the process generally called 'learning'—if he is strenuous and does not faint; for all inquiry and all learning is but recollection. (81a-d)

Timaeus

Oceanus and Tethys were the children of Earth and Heaven, and from these sprang Phorcys and Cronos and Rhea, and all that generation; and from Cronos and Rhea sprang Zeus and Hera, and all those who are said to be their brethren, and others who were the children of these.

Now, when all of them, both those who visibly appear in their revolutions as well as those other gods who are of a more retiring nature, had come into being, the creator of the universe addressed them in these words: 'Gods, children of gods, who are my works, and of whom I am the artificer and father, my creations are indissoluble, if so I will. All that is bound may be undone, but only an evil being would wish to undo that which is harmonious and happy. Wherefore, since ye are but creatures, ye are not altogether immortal and indissoluble, but ye shall certainly not be dissolved, nor be liable to the fate of death, having in my will a greater and mightier bond than those with which ye were bound at the time of your birth. And now listen to my instructions:—Three tribes of mortal beings remain to be created—without them the universe will be incomplete, for it will not contain every kind of animal which it ought to contain, if it is to be perfect. On the other hand, if they were created by me and received life at my hands, they would be on an equality with the gods. In order then that they may be mortal, and that this universe may be truly universal, do ye, according to your natures, betake yourselves to the formation of animals, imitating the power which was shown by me in creating you. The part of them worthy of the name immortal, which is called divine and is the guiding principle of those who are willing to follow justice and you—of that divine part I will myself sow the seed, and having made a beginning, I will hand the work over to you. And do ye then interweave the mortal with the immortal, and make and beget living creatures, and give them food, and make them to grow, and receive them again in death.' (40e-41d)

The Laws

Thus a man is born and brought up, and after this manner he begets and brings up his own children, and has his share of dealings with other men, and suffers if he has done wrong to anyone, and receives satisfaction if he has been wronged, and so at length in due time he grows old under the protection of the laws, and his end comes in the order of nature. Concerning the dead of either sex, the religious ceremonies which may fittingly be performed, whether appertaining to the gods of the under-world or of this, shall be decided by the interpreters with absolute authority. Their sepulchres are not to be in places which are fit for cultivation, and there shall be no monuments in such spots, either large or small, but they shall occupy that part of the country which is naturally adapted for receiving and concealing the bodies of the dead with as little hurt as possible to the living. No man, living or dead, shall deprive the living of the sustenance which the earth, their foster-parent, is naturally inclined to provide for them. And let not the mound be piled higher than would be the work of five men completed in five days; nor shall the stone which is placed over the spot be larger than would be sufficient to receive the praises of the dead included in four heroic lines. Nor shall the laying out of the dead in the house continue for a longer time than is sufficient to distinguish between him who is in a trance only and him who is really dead, and speaking generally, the third day after death will be a fair time for carrying out the body to the sepulchre. Now we must believe the legislator when he tells us that the soul is in all respects superior to the body, and that even in life what makes each one of us to be what we are is only the soul; and that the body follows us about in the likeness of each of us, and therefore, when we are dead, the bodies of the dead are quite rightly said to be our shades or images; for the true and immortal being of each one of us which is called the soul goes on her way to other gods, before them to give an account—which is an inspiring hope to the good, but very terrible to the bad—as the laws of our fathers tell us; and they also say that not much can be done in the way of helping a man after he is dead. But the living—he should be helped by all his kindred, that while in life he may be the holiest and justest of men, and after death may have no great sins to be punished in the world below. If this be true, a man ought not to waste his substance under the idea that all this lifeless mass of flesh which is in process of burial is connected with him; he should consider that the son, or brother, or the beloved one, whoever he may be, whom he thinks he is laying in the earth, has gone away to complete and fulfil his own destiny, and that his duty is rightly to order the present, and to spend moderately on the lifeless altar of the gods below. But the legislator does not intend moderation to be taken in the sense of meanness. Let the law, then, be as follows:—The expenditure on the entire funeral of him who is of the highest class shall not exceed five minas; and for him who is of the second class, three minas, and for him who is of the third class, two minas, and for him who is of the fourth class, one mina, will be a fair limit of expense. The guardians of the law, who are responsible for so much else, must take especial care of each successive age of life; and at the end of all, let there be some one guardian of the law presiding, who shall be chosen by the friends of the deceased to superintend, and let it be glory to him to manage with fairness and moderation what relates to the dead, and a discredit to him if they are not well managed. Let the laying out and other ceremonies be in accordance with custom, but to the statesman who adopts custom as his law we must give way in certain particulars. It would be monstrous for example that he should command any man to weep or abstain from weeping over the dead; but he may forbid cries of lamentation, and not allow the voice of the mourner to be heard outside the house; also, he may forbid the bringing of the dead body into the open streets, or the processions of mourners in the streets, and may require that before daybreak they should be outside the city. Let these, then, be our laws relating to such matters . . . (Book XII, 958c-960a)

ARISTOTLE

On Youth, Old Age, Life and Death, and Respiration

1 . We must now treat of youth and old age and life and death. We must probably also at the same time state the causes of respiration as well, since in some cases living and the reverse depend on this.

We have elsewhere given an account of the soul, and while it is clear that its substance cannot be corporeal, yet manifestly it must exist in some bodily part which must be one of those possessing control over the members. Let us for the present set aside the other parts or faculties of the soul (whichever of the two be the correct name). But as to being what is called an animal and a living thing, we find that in all beings endowed with both characteristics (viz. being an animal and being alive) there must be a single identical part in virtue of which they live and are called animals; for an animal *qua* animal cannot avoid being alive. But a thing need not, though alive, be animal; for plants live without having sensation, and it is by sensation that we distinguish animal from what is not animal . . .

Democritus, however, does teach that in the breathing animals there is a certain result produced by respiration; he asserts that it prevents the soul from being extruded from the body. Nevertheless, he by no means asserts that it is for this purpose that nature so contrives it, for he, like the other natural scientists, altogether fails to attain to any such explanation. His statement is that the soul and the hot element are identical, being the primary forms among the spherical particles. Hence, when these are being separated out by the surrounding atmosphere thrusting them out, respiration, according to his account, comes in to succour them. For in the air there are many of those particles which he calls mind and soul. Hence, when we breathe and the air enters, these enter along with it, and by their action cancel the pressure, thus preventing the expulsion of the soul which resides in the animal.

The explains why life and death are bound up with the taking in and letting out of the breath; for death occurs when the compression by the surrounding air gains the upper hand, and, the animal being unable to respire, the air from outside can no longer enter and counteract the compression. Death is the departure of those forms owing to the expulsive pressure exerted by the surrounding air. As to the reason why all must die at some time—not, however, at any chance time but, when natural, owing to old age, and, when unnatural, to violence.

But the reason for this and why all must die Democritus has by no means made clear. And yet, since evidently death occurs at one time of life and not at another, he should have said whether the cause is external or internal . . . (467b10-25; 471b30-472a20)

To be born and to die are common to all animals, but there are specifically diverse ways in which these phenomena occur; of destruction there are different types, though yet something is common to them all. There is violent death and again natural death, and the former occurs when the cause of death is external, the latter when it is internal, and involved from the beginning in the constitution of the organ, and not an affection derived from a foreign source. In the case of plants the name given to this is withering, in animals old age. Death and decay pertain to all things that are not imperfectly developed; to the imperfect also they may be ascribed in nearly the same but not an identical sense. Under the imperfect I class eggs and seeds of plants as they are before the root appears.

It is always to some lack of heat that death is due, and in perfect creatures the cause is its failure in the organ containing the source of the creature's essential nature. This member is sited, as has been said, at the junction of the upper and lower parts; in plants it is intermediate between the root and the stem, in sanguineous animals it is the heart, and in those that are bloodless the corresponding part of their body. But some of these animals have potentially many sources of life, though in actuality they possess only one. This is why some insects live when divided, and why, even among sanguineous animals, all whose vitality is not intense live for a long time after the heart has been removed. Tortoises, for example, do so and make movements with their feet, so long as the shell is left, a fact to be explained by the natural inferiority of their constitution, as it is in insects also.

The source of life is lost to its possessors when the heat with which it is bound up is no longer tempered by cooling, for, as I have often remarked, it is consumed by itself. Hence when, owing to lapse of time, the lung in the one class and the gills in the other get dried up, these organs become hard and earthy and incapable of movement and cannot be expanded or contracted. Finally things come to a climax, and the fire goes out from exhaustion.

Hence a small disturbance will speedily cause death in old age. Little heat remains, for the most of it has been breathed away in the long period of life preceding, and hence any increase of strain on the organ quickly causes extinction. It is just as though the heart contained a tiny feeble flame which the slightest movement puts out. Hence in old age death is painless, for no violent disturbance is required to cause death, and the severance of the soul is entirely imperceptible. All diseases which harden the lung by forming tumours or waste residues, or by excess of morbid heat, as happens in fevers, accelerate the breathing owing to the inability of the lung to move far either upwards or downwards. Finally, when motion is no longer possible, the breath is given out and death ensues.

Generation is the initial participation, mediated by warm substance, in the nutritive soul, and life is the maintenance of this participation. Youth is the period of the growth of the primary organ of refrigeration, old age of its decay, while the intervening time is the prime of life.

A violent death or dissolution consists in the extinction or exhaustion of the vital heat (for either of these may cause dissolution), while natural death is the exhaustion of the heat owing to lapse of time, and occurring at the end of life. In plants this is to wither, in animals to die. Death, in old age, is the exhaustion due to inability on the part of the organ, owing to old age, to produce refrigeration.

This then is our account of generation and life and death, and the reason for their occurrence in animals. (478b22-479b7)

On Length and Shortness of Life

1. The reasons for some animals being long-lived and others short-lived, and, in a word, the causes of the length and brevity of life call for investigation.

The necessary beginning to our inquiry is a statement of the difficulties about these points. For it is not clear whether in animals and plants universally it is a single or diverse cause that makes some to be long-lived, others short-lived. Plants too have in some cases a long life, while in others it lasts but for a year.

Further, in a natural structure are longevity and a sound constitution coincident, or is shortness of life independent of unhealthiness? Perhaps in the case of certain maladies a diseased state of the body and shortness of life are interchangeable, while in the case of others ill-health is perfectly compatible with long life.

Of sleep and waking we have already treated; about life and death we shall speak later on, and likewise about health and disease, in so far as it belongs to the science of nature to do so. But at present we have to investigate the causes of some creatures being long-lived, others short-lived as we have said before. We find this distinction affecting not only entire genera opposed as wholes to one another, but applying also to contrasted sets of individuals within the same species. As an instance of the difference applying to the genus I give man and horse (for mankind has a longer life than the horse), while within the species there is the difference between man and man; for of men also some are long-lived, others short-lived, differing from each other in respect of the different regions in which they dwell. Races inhabiting warm countries have longer life, those living in a cold climate live a shorter time. Likewise these are similar differences among individuals occupying the same locality.

2. We must answer the question, What is that which, in natural objects, makes them easily destroyed, or the reverse? Since fire and water, and whatsoever is akin thereto, do not possess identical powers they are reciprocal causes of generation and decay. Hence it is natural to infer that everything else arising from them and composed of them should share in the same nature, in all cases where things are not, like a house, a composite unity formed by the synthesis of many things.

In other matters a different account must be given; for in many things their mode of dissolution is something peculiar to themselves, e.g. in knowledge and ignorance, health and disease. These pass away even though the medium in which they are found is not destroyed but continues to exist; for example, take the termination of ignorance, which

is recollection or learning, while knowledge passes away into forgetfulness, or error. But accidentally the disintegration of a natural object is
accompanied by the destruction of the other things; for, when the
animal dies, the health or knowledge resident in it passes away too.
Hence from these considerations we may draw a conclusion about the
soul too; for, if the inherence of soul in body is not a matter of nature but
like that of knowledge in the soul, there would be another mode of
dissolution pertaining to it besides that which occurs when the body is
destroyed. But since evidently it does not admit of this dual dissolution,
the soul must stand in a different case in respect of its union with the
body.

3. Perhaps one might reasonably raise the question whether there is
any place where what is corruptible becomes incorruptible, as fire does
in the upper regions where it meets with no opposite. Opposites destroy
each other, and hence accidentally, by their destruction, whatsoever is
attributed to them is destroyed. But no opposite in a real substance is
accidentally destroyed, because real substance is no⁺ predicated of any
subject. Hence a thing which has no opposite, or which is situated where
it has no opposite, cannot be destroyed. For what will that be which can
destroy it, if destruction comes only through contraries, but no contrary
to it exists either absolutely or in the particular place where it is? But
perhaps this is in one sense true, in another sense not true, for it is
impossible that anything containing matter should not have in any sense
an opposite. Heat and straightness can be present in every part of a
thing, but it is impossible that the thing should be nothing but hot or
white or straight; for, if that were so, attributes would have a separate
existence. Hence if, in all cases, whenever the active and the passive exist
together, the one acts and the other is acted on, it is impossible that no
change should occur. Further, this is so if a waste product is an opposite,
and waste must always be produced; for opposition is always the source
of change, and waste is what remains of the previous opposite. But, after
expelling everything of a nature actually opposed, an object would in
this case also be imperishable. Or would it be destroyed by the environment?

If then that is so, what we have said sufficiently accounts for the
change; but, if not, we must assume that something of actually opposite
character is in the changing object, and waste is produced.

Hence accidentally a lesser flame is consumed by a greater one, for the
nutriment, to wit the smoke, which the former takes a long period to
expend, is used up by the big flame quickly.

Hence all things are at all times in a state of transition and are coming into being or passing away. The environment acts on them either favourably or antagonistically, and, owing to this, things that change their situation become more or less enduring than their nature warrants, but never are they eternal when they contain contrary qualities; for their matter is an immediate source of contrariety, so that if it involves locality they show change of situation, if quantity, increase and diminution, while if it involves qualitative affection we find alteration of character.

4. We find that a superior immunity from decay attaches neither to the largest animals (the horse has shorter life than man) nor to those that are small (for many insects live but for a year). Nor are plants as a whole less liable to perish than animals (many plants are annuals), nor have sanguineous animals the pre-eminence (for the bee is longer-lived than certain sanguineous animals). Neither is it the bloodless animals that live longest (for molluscs live only a year, though bloodless), nor terrestrial organisms (there are both plants and terrestrial animals of which a single year is the period), nor the occupants of the sea (for there we find the crustaceans and the molluscs, which are short-lived).

Speaking generally, the longest-lived things occur among the plants, e.g. the date-palm. Next in order we find them among the sanguineous animals rather than among the bloodless, and among land animals rather than among water animals. Hence, taking these two characters together, the longest-lived animals fall among sanguineous land animals, e.g. man and elephant. As a matter of fact also it is a general rule that the larger live longer than the smaller, for the other long-lived animals too happen to be of a large size, as are also those I have mentioned.

5. The following considerations may enable us to understand the reasons for all these facts. We must remember that an animal is by nature humid and warm, and to live is to be of such a constitution, while old age is dry and cold, and so is a corpse. This is plain to observation. But the material constituting the bodies of all animals consists of the following—the hot and the cold, the dry and the moist. Hence when they age they must become dry, and therefore the fluid in them requires to be not easily dried up. Thus we explain why fat things are not liable to decay. The reason is that they contain air; now air relatively to the other elements is fire, and fire never becomes rotten.

Again the humid element in animals must not be small in quantity, for a small quantity is easily dried up. This is why both plants and animals that are large are, as a general rule, longer-lived than the rest, as was said before; it is to be expected that the larger should contain more moisture. But it is not merely this that makes them longer lived; for the cause is twofold, to wit, the quality as well as the quantity of the fluid. Hence the moisture must be not only great in amount but also warm, in order to be neither easily congealed nor easily dried up.

It is for this reason also that man lives longer than some animals which are larger; for animals live longer though there is a deficiency in the amount of their moisture, if the ratio of its qualitative superiority exceeds that of its quantitative deficiency.

In some creatures the warm element is their fatty substance, which prevents at once desiccation and cooling; but in others it assumes a different flavour. Further, that which is designed to be not easily destroyed should not yield waste products. Anything of such a nature causes death either by disease or naturally, for the potency of the waste product works adversely and destroys now the entire constitution, now a particular member.

This is why animals that copulate frequently and those abounding in seed age quickly; the seed is a residue, and further, by being lost, it produces dryness. Hence the mule lives longer than either the horse or the ass from which it sprang, and females live longer than males if the males copulate frequently. Accordingly cock-sparrows have a shorter life than the females. Again males subject to great toil are short-lived and age more quickly owing to the labour; toil produces dryness and old age is dry. But by natural constitution and as a general rule males live longer than females, and the reason is that the male is an animal with more warmth than the female.

The same kind of animals are longer-lived in warm than in cold climates for the same reason as they are of larger size. The size of animals of cold constitution illustrates this particularly well, and hence snakes and lizards and scaly reptiles are of great size in warm localities, as also are testacea in the Red Sea: the warm humidity there is the cause equally of their augmented size and of their life. But in cold countries the humidity in animals is more of a watery nature, and hence is readily congealed. Consequently it happens that animals with little or no blood are in northerly regions either entirely absent (both land and water animals) or, when they do occur, they are smaller and have shorter life; for the frost prevents growth.

Both plants and animals perish if not fed, for in that case they consume themselves; just as a large flame consumes and burns up a small one by using up its nutriment, so the natural warmth which is the primary cause of digestion consumes the material in which it is located.

Water animals have a shorter life than terrestrial creatures, not strictly because they are humid, but because they are watery, and watery moisture is easily destroyed, since it is cold and readily congealed. For the same reason bloodless animals perish readily unless protected by great size, for there is neither fatness nor sweetness about them. In animals fat is sweet, and hence bees are longer-lived than other animals of larger size. (464b20-467a5)

CHAPTER 2
Oriental Attitudes Toward Death:
An Overview

Oriental sages persuade us repeatedly that it is sheer delusion to take death as life-negation; death has something *positive* for us, on three counts: (1) Death is part of life; (2) Death ends life; and (3) Death continues life.

(1) Death is taken to be part of life, especially in China. The dead ancestors are profoundly alive, blessing their living posterity with good life, and receiving honors and gifts from them. This is ancestor worship, reverently endorsed by Confucius and the Confucians. Then there are the Taoists, who see death as life's complement; death starts a new round of existence. The ancient Greeks, as we have seen, also thought that life continues after death, but Confucius thinks less of our death than of the dead ancestors impinging on us, the living, giving us continual protection and blessings in return for our continual sacrifices, offerings, and upkeep of their abodes, the graves.

(2) Death is taken to end life. The neo-Confucians take life to be a congregation of vital energies (as Empedocles and Aristotle did), while the Buddhists take life to be an aggregate of elements which in turn arise out of our ignorance. Such a gathering should be expected to disperse in due course.

Some Japanese take death to be what gives the finishing touch to life, thereby determining life's value. All that ends well has fared well; we must then make sure that we live in such a way that life can end well. In contrast, the Buddhists take the ending of life to symbolize the vacuity of things.

(3) Finally, death is taken to continue life in a radically different, ultimate manner. The Tibetan Buddhists think so (as did Pythagoras), and so do the Hindus; when the virtuous die they become one with the One, the Ground of reality.

All these views hold that, although a serious matter, death is not evil unless *we* make it so (as Socrates and the Pythagorean preparations for dying assume). Death is even regarded as a good in Buddhism; the death of our beloved prods us into gaining enlightenment, awakening us from the delusion of ignorance about how things are. In our ignorance we take things to be really there, when, despite appearances, things are *really* vacuous.

Thus we have in the Orient three traditions holding different views on death—the Chinese, the Hindu, and the Buddhist (with Tibetan Buddhist).

1. The *Chinese* tradition has two schools—Confucianism and Taoism. First we consider Confucius and the Confucians.

Confucius was born in the tumultuous age of ancient China (551–497). He was more intent on death's impact on us, especially our attitude toward the dead ancestors, than on the nature of death itself. Perhaps he thought that nothing is more educative of life than training our feelings, our attitudes, and our conduct in face of the ultimate—death and the dead. And so reverence toward the dead ancestors was of paramount importance to him, both as our extension of filial love and as our self-cultivation.

Asked about death, he answered, "Not yet knowing life, how can I know death?" (11/12). This famous saying can mean that only those who live reverently can grow in their reverent understanding of death, the ultimate matter of life. We must, then, cease idle speculation about death and conduct ourselves properly in life; thus we will come to understand death in due course.

How do we reconcile Confucius' ritualized sorrow at the funeral with his endorsement of ancestor worship which implies that the ancestors live on? Perhaps Chinese common sense is at work here. It is *natural* to feel sad at our ancestors' death; it is *natural*, given our reverence, to presume that they live on to protect us. And for their protection, we provide them with honor, food and abodes (graves). There is no contradiction here; even our sorrow is part of our reverence. And our reverence, as Mencius emphasizes, enhances our personal integrity.

Our selections on Confucius are from *The Analects,* translated by Kuang-ming Wu. Our selections on the Confucians are as follows: that on Mencius (371–289?) is from *Mencius,* translated by Kuang-ming Wu, that on Hsun Tzu (fl. 298–238) is from Burton Watson's translation in *Basic Writings of Hsun Tzu.* Selections on the Neo-Confucians are as follows; that on Wang Ch'ung (27–100?) is from Burton Watson's translation in Cyril Birch, ed., *Anthology of Chinese Literature,* that on Yang Hsiung (53 BC–AD 18) is from Wing-tsit Chan's translation in *A Source Book in Chinese Philosophy,* and that on Ch'eng I (1033–1107) is also from Wing-tsit Chan's translation in the same book.

The Taoists say that our fear of death comes from believing death is the taker of life, as something separate from and opposed to life. We think that there is no death in life, no life in death; we link love with life, hatred with death. Yet in fact life and death co-exist; one does not exist without the other, the one leading to the other. Our mortal fear disappears as we take life and death to be complementary.

Lao Tzu, a legendary sage and supposed contemporary of Confucius, was reputed to have ridden an ox out of the city gate instead of dying. He says that death is part of life, and life is part of death—both originate in the Female Gate of heaven and earth. Clinging to life brings death; *inflexible* clinging itself is a sign of death. We must live without a craving for life, and then we can die without dying; we will be as placid as that Female Gate, and as pliable as the Infant.

It is well known that his sayings are obscure, so much so that an elaborate interpretive tradition has arisen concerning what this or that passage means. It is safe to say that Lao Tzu's collected sayings do not describe or designate, much less do they enunciate eternal truths. Rather, they are incantatory, meant to sink into the reader, whose own thoughtful exploration they thereby evoke. It is therefore not only otiose but misguided to say categorically what Lao Tzu really meant in this or that passage. But it is helpful to provide some implications of some obscure phrases, and thereby render the modern Western reader contemporaneous with the ancient thought world of Lao Tzu.

"Valley" in Chapter Six symbolizes whatever is ruggedly natural that is hollow, accepting, and below, thanks to which whatever is mountainous stands out as such. "The spirit of the valley dies not," because only the mountainous die; the valley is what makes possible the mountainous. And this is equivalent to the Gate of the Female—empty, accommodating, through which things come into being.

"Thirteen" in Chapter Fifty can mean also three tenth, that is, one third, meaning perhaps those who are rash enough to tend to the extremities of life and death are respectively one third of the people at large. What is required of us is to stay in the middle road. Or else one can take "thirteen" to mean "four limbs and nine bodily hollows" (our bodily life), "the rise and fall of the five elementary ways of the universe" (the vicissitudes of life), and so on. Thus taken, the same elements (whether bodily or natural) are sometimes the companions of life, sometimes those of death. To preserve life one must be oneself, worrying about nothing, depending on nothing. How can one fully be oneself? Learn the crucial art of life from the infant, as adumbrated in Chapter Fifty-Five.

Chapters Seventy-Four through Seventy-Six apply the above life principle to management of the people—do not play God by ruthlessly driving people to the limits of their patience; life is soft and death hard, and so the ruler must follow life's way and be tender and accommodating with the people. Our selections from Lao Tzu's *Tao Te Ching* are translated by Kuang-ming Wu.

Chuang Tzu (fourth century B.C., a contemporary of Mencius) tells us that we can affirm the value of living, in fact, joyously roaming in the world of change as long as we leave its frets and worries alone. Such joyous affirmation enables us to look forward to the afterlife, whatever it is, to which death is the gate. If Lao Tzu wants us to accept death calmly, avoiding the death-like inflexibility and fixation, Chuang Tzu positively revels in death which is part of the constant changes of the universal Way of things.

Although both Taoists are evocative, Lao Tzu is enigmatic and epigrammatic while Chuang Tzu is hilarious, always ready with witty stories.

Let us take an example from "perfect happiness," where Chuang Tzu had a dream conversation with a skull at the roadside. Not believing in the skull's confession about its invincible self-enjoyment, Chuang Tzu asked if it wanted him to ask the Arbiter of Fate to restore its former life with its body, family and friend. "The skull frowned severely, wrinkling up its brow. 'Why would I throw away more happiness than that of a king on a throne and take on the troubles of a human being again?'"

Its joy is as strange as it is natural: "Among the dead there are no rulers above, no subjects below, and no chores of the four seasons. With nothing to do, our springs and autumns are as endless as heaven and earth. A king facing south on his throne could have no more happiness than this!"

To die at the roadside is the most disgraceful of all manners of human life in China, as Mencius often mentioned (cf. 3A5). Chuang Tzu chose that precise manner of being, the rock bottom to which anyone can go, and endowed it with the joy that no one can take away. That dry skull sits (?) at the roadside, and no devil (if any), much less vultures, wolves, earthworms, would take a second look at it; no one would care to touch it, much less harm it.

And yet the skull is not insignificant. For there cannot be a roadside skull-in-general; the skull is unmistakably that of a particular individual; it is "mine." Being the rock bottom to which I can go, I as that dry skull am invincible, sharing the happy rounds of seasons with the heaven and earth. And I carry that skull, alive or dead; I can enjoy my life as the skull enjoys its existence, season after season. This is what Chuang Tzu called "perfect happiness," whether I am alive or dead. The selections from Chuang Tzu are taken from Burton Watson's translations in *The Complete Works of Chuang Tzu.*

2. The Hindu tradition says that behind the rounds of births and deaths, rebirths and redeaths, is that One, that Atman (the ultimate self), that Brahman (the objective ultimate), which is a neither-nor, completely indescribable and unfixable in every way. To go back to *that* is "immortality."

We see three points here. First, the goddess of Death is the goddess of justice *(dharma),* who represents the Hindu belief in *karma,* desert-formation by life-performance, that is, to perform in life is to form one's desert in the after-life. As one sows deeds in life, so one reaps one's deserved reward or punishment in the after-life. Neither death nor any other punishment (or reward) is inflicted by an external agency, but is merely the deed recoiling upon its agent, as Plato's "myth of Er" also proclaimed. The wicked suffer in eternal darkness below for their wickedness; the virtuous enjoy happiness in bright heaven above with the gods.

All this points, secondly, to the immortality of the soul. Death is not destruction but existence continuing elsewhere, where happiness or misery ensues as one's *karma* deserves.

Finally, the above beliefs alert us to our conduct in *this* life. We prepare, as the Pythagoreans did, for the ideal beyond, which is none other than *what* reaches it; the craved for Braham (ideal) is none other than Atman, the self purified from the delusion of duality of the me and the not-me. Salvation *(moksa)* is eternal bliss *(ananda)* beyond duality, the origin of all strife.

One is tempted here to speculate on what *sort* of reincarnation the Hindus assume for the soul after death, how their concept of transmigration differs from the ancient Greeks, and the like. There have been as many views of transmigration as there are cultures and religions—the primitive, the Celtic, the Egyptian, the Buddhist, and the list goes on. One thing is certain—they all enjoin us to live our lives properly so as to prepare ourselves for the after-life, whatever it is.

The Hindu readings are represented by the orthodox tradition (the *Upanishads*) and the heterodox tradition, Buddhism. Our selections from the *Upanishads* are taken from Robert Ernest Hume's translations in *The Thirteen Principal Upanishads.* Our selections from Buddhism are from Henry Clarke Warren, ed., *Buddhism in Translations.*

3. The Buddhist tradition says that to extinguish the desire of "me" and "mine" and become indifferent, as a man's feelings toward his ex-wife (that is, his former bodily elements that constituted "himself")—this is Nirvana, without consciousness, without rebirth.

What prevents the self from the freedom from rounds of births and deaths is *karma*—the deposited formations of one's performances in life, born of the self's *desire* to cling on to the illusory possessions, one of which is the notion of the "self." All disciplines and meditations are for the sake of eradicating all such desires, of awakening oneself from illusion.

As for Zen Buddhism, already too much has been written on it, mostly textual, historical, and anecdotal. Zen has two remarkable traits; it is practical, and it is a blend of insights of three cultures, Hindu, Chinese, and Japanese.

First, it is practical in the sense that it only tells the stories of the enlightenment and the ease of the enlightened daily ongoings, not the rationale and explanation of such living. Reading Zen writings feels like taking a bus trip without knowing how the bus works or how to drive it. What is important is to practice until one gains Zen-satori, the enlightenment, not its mechanics and rationale.

Secondly, Zen is a blend of three cultural traditions and insights. Although our selections are from Chinese sources dealing with Buddhistic insights (from India), these sources are quoted reverently by Japanese Zen Masters. The term "Zen" is the Japanese pronunciation of the Chinese "ch'an," which, in turn, is the Chinese pronunciation of the Indian "dhyana." Hence to quote from the Chinese sources is to delve into the peculiarities of Zen as it evolved from one culture to another, incorporating and digesting (transforming) whatever sentiments and insights Zen Buddhists picked up in the course of their religious-cultural-thought evolution.

For the Zennist, the One Reality underlies life vicissitudes (Hindu); the Ultimate One is called Nothing, Nirvana, Nameless (Buddhist); living according to this view is called natural, going along with nature (Taoist); and at any moment one can die with an absolute ease (Japanese). In short, Zen Buddhism is a pragmatic synthesis of the Oriental sentiment.

Oriental pragmatism is crystallized in the Zen habitation in the "suchness" of what there is, the fullness of the here and now, which is all too often smothered in various connections with the future (plans and worries) and with the past (guilts and glories). The so-called Zen koans are Zen masters' many irrelevant (often painfully rude) answers to important questions about the essence of Buddha. The very irrelevance jolts us, awakening us to the fullness of the present.

Let us take an example. To the question, "What is the meaning of our Master [Dharma] coming from the West? (Why did he come? How significant for us is his coming?)," Master Chao-chou Ts'ung-shen replied, "That cypress tree in the yard."

Buddha (or Buddhism, Nirvana, Enlightenment) is not a person in the past, about whose relation to us we can ask and discuss. Nor is Buddhism an esoteric essence of truth to be abstracted from the daily hustle and bustle. This denial ("not," "nor") of historical connection and logical speculation is expressed in the sudden irrelevance of the answer that points to the familiar tree in the yard, that tree on which the master's eye happened to rest at the moment, that "here and now." For that moment, absolutely full and alive, is the moment of Buddha, literally an awakening that is lived. The Master's words here (and sometimes a rude slapping or beating) do not refer and explain; they express the exigencies of the here and now, whose fullness is thereby thrust forth, opening our entire selves toward it.

This sort of raw full contact with the fullness and intensity of the present, at which we have no time for logic or history or sense, deprives death of its sting of fear. We can now taste, even revel in, the fullness of the cessation of life, here and now.

Our selection from Zen Buddhism is from Christopher Cleary's translations in *Swampland Flowers: The Letters and Lectures of Zen Master Ta Hui.*

Tibetan Buddhism is another curious blend of Hindu and Buddhist insights. Bardos (existential gaps and uncertainties) in and after life must be eliminated by meditations and chants, so that we can journey on without illusion (Buddhist) in the after-life, after-death world, for a better and more complete existence (Hindu).

Our selections on Tibetan Buddhism are taken from W. Y. Evans-Wentz, *The Tibetan Book of the Dead* and Francesca Frenantle & Chogyam Trunga, *The Tibetan Book of the Dead.*

In short, what we find in this chapter is that death is generally given a positive value for the present life. We live rightly to enjoy the beyond. The distinctions among the various traditions are concerned with what living "rightly" consists of, and what such "enjoyment" amounts to.

References

Chan, Wing Tsit, tr. *A Source Book of Chinese Philosophy.* Princeton: Princeton University Press, 1963, p. 290, 564.

Cleary, Christopher, tr. *Swampland Flowers: The Letters and Lectures of Zen Master Ta Hui.* NY: Grove Press, 1977, pp. xx, 78.

Confucius, *The Analects,* tr. Kuang-Ming Wu, 1987, 2/5, 3/4, 8/4, 11/11, 12/5, 15/9, 17/21, 19/1.

Evans-Wenz, W. Y., ed., *The Tibetan Book of the Dead*. Oxford: Oxford University Press, 1960, pp. 163–165.

Fremantle, Francesca and Chogyam Trungpa, *The Tibetan Book of the Dead*. Boston: Shambhala Publications, 1975, pp. 1–2, 98–99.

Hsun Tzu, *The Basic Writings of Hsun Tzu*. tr. Burton Watson, NY: Columbia University Press, 1967, pp. 96–97.

Hume, Robert Ernest, tr., *The Thirteen Principal Upanishads*. NY: Oxford University Press, 1896, pp. 76, 89–91, 162–63, 224, 267, 303, 364, 365, 384, 389–90, 396, 405.

Lao Tzu, *Tao Te Ching*, tr. Kuang-Ming Wu, 1987, Chapters 6, 33, 50, 55, 74–76.

Mencius, *Mencius*, tr. Kuang-Ming Wu, 1987, 6A10.

Warren, Henry Clark, ed. *Buddhism in Translations*. Cambridge: Harvard University Press, 1896, pp. 133–134, 146, 148, 149, 232–33, 252–53, 255–56, 258, 259, 276–77, 378–79, 380, 387–88, 389.

Watson, Burton tr., in Cyril Birch ed., *Anthology of Chinese Literature*. NY: Grove Press, 1965, pp. 88–90.

Watson, Burton tr. *The Complete Works of Chung Tzu*. NY: Columbia University Press, 1968. pp. 36, 37, 47, 52–53, 73–74, 78, 80, 82–83, 83–87, 88–89, 144, 168–169, 191–194, 195, 235, 238, 239, 240, 241, 242, 245–46, 293, 373–74, 361.

The Chinese Tradition

CONFUCIUS

The Analects

2:5: Meng I Tzu asked about filial love. The Master said, "No disobedience." . . . Fan Ch'ih said, "What do you mean?" The Master said, "While parents are alive, serve them with the rites of honor; when dead, bury with the rites of honor, sacrifice to them with the rites of honor."

3:4: Lin Fang asked about the root of the rites of honor. The Master said, "Great indeed is the question! The rites of honor in general require less excess than restraint. [For example,] funeral requires less wailing than grieving."

8:4: Master Tseng was sick. Meng Ching Tzu inquired after him. Master Tseng mumbled, saying, "Birds about to die, their cries are touching; men about to die, their sayings are worthy."

11:11: Chi Lu asked about serving the ghosts and divinities. The Master said, "[Not] yet able to serve men, how can we serve ghosts?" He said, "I venture to ask about death." "[Not] yet knowing about life, how can we know about death?"

12:5: Ssu-ma Niu was distressed, saying, "People all have brothers; I alone have none." Tzu-hsia said, "I overheard it [said], 'Death and life are decreed; wealth and nobility are up to the Heaven. Gentlemen do not fail to be reverent, [and] are courteous and honorable with people; all within the Four Seas are [then] brothers.' How can a gentleman worry about having no brothers?"

15:8: The Master said, "No knightly knight or humanly man will seek life and injure humanness. On the contrary, there are some who killed their bodies to realize humanness."

17:21: Tsai Wo asked about three years' mourning [period], saying, "One year is already too long. Let gentlemen for three years not practice the rites of honor, and the rites will surely be in ruins. Let them for three years not practice music, and music will surely crumble. The old grains having been used up, the new ones being on the rise, and the round of the change of firewoods having been completed, one year is already long enough."

The Master said, "Are you [then after a year] at ease eating [good] rice and wearing silk embroideries?" He said, "[Quite] at ease." "If you are at ease, then do so. But the gentleman stays in mourning; eating delicacies he does not relish them, hearing music he does not enjoy it, residing at [the usual] place he is not at ease, and so he does not do [these things]. Now that you are at ease, do so."

Tsai Wo went. The Master said, "O, the inhumanness of Yu! A child after birth must pass three years before being relieved of the parents' bosom. Three years' mourning is the common mourning [period] under heaven. Alas, Yu, did you [not] have three years of love at your parents'?"

19:1: Tzu-chang said, "The knight, seeing danger, [is prepared to] put his life to [the task]; seeing gain, [he] thinks of righteousness; in sacrifice, [he] thinks reverently; in funeral, [he] thinks mournfully—such a one is all that can be desired."

Mencius: 6A10

Mencius said, "Fish is what I desire; bear's paws are also what I desire. If the two cannot both be obtained, I give up fish and take bear's paws. Similarly, life is what I desire; righteousness is also what I desire. If the two cannot both be obtained, [I] give up life and take righteousness. Although life is also what I desire, [I] have something more desirable than life; therefore, [I] do not improperly obtain it. Although death is what I detest, [I] have something more detestable than death; therefore, suffering [it I] do not avoid.

Had men nothing more desirable than life, then whatever [means] to obtain life why don't [they] use? Had men nothing more detestable than death, then whatever [to be done] to avoid suffering [it] why don't they do? From this, [and observing that] there have been [men who,] having [means of] living [or] avoiding death, did not use [them, we conclude that] therefore there is in what [we] desire something more [desirable] than life, in what [we] detest something more [detestable] than death. Not only do worthy ones have this [type of] mind; all men have it. Worthy ones merely manage not to lose [it].

A basket of food, a bowl of soup—get them, and one lives; do not get them, and one dies. Scream at someone and give them, [then] not a tramp would receive them. Trample upon the foods and give them, [then] not a beggar would stoop to take them.

If, [being offered] myriads of *chung* [of emolument], I receive it without considering the rites of honor and righteousness—what do myriads of *chung* add on me? Is it because of the beauty of [my] mansions, the services of [my] wives and concubines, what [my] poverty-stricken acquaintances can get out of me? Before, [even] at the cost of [my] bodily death [I] did not receive [the benefit]; now [I] receive [it] because of beautiful mansions, ladies' services, poor friends. Is this [because I now] cannot help [it]? This it is which is called 'losing one's original mind.'"

The *Hsun Tzu*
(from *Hsun Tzu: Basic Writings*)

Rites are strictest in their ordering of birth and death. Birth is the beginning of man, death his end. When both beginning and end are good, man's way is complete. Therefore the gentleman is reverent in his treatment of the beginning and careful in his treatment of the end, regarding both with the same gravity. This is the way of the gentleman and the highest flowering of ritual principle. To be generous in the treatment of the living but skimpy in the treatment of the dead is to show reverence for a being who has consciousness and contempt for one who has lost it. This is the way of an evil man and an offense against the heart. The gentleman would be ashamed to treat even a lowly slave in a way that offends the heart; how much more ashamed would he be to treat those whom he honors and loves in such a way! The rites of the dead can be performed only once for each individual, and never again. They are the last occasion upon which the subject may fully express respect for his ruler, the son express respect for his parents.

Wang Ch'ung
(from *Anthology of Chinese Literature*)

A Discussion of Death
[*Lun heng,* XX]

People say that when men die they become ghosts with consciousness and the power to harm others. If we try to test this theory by comparing men with other creatures, however, we find that men do not become ghosts, nor do they have consciousness or power to harm. . . . Man lives because of his vital force *(ch'i)* and when he dies this vital force is extinguished. The vital force is able to function because of the blood system, but when a man dies the blood system ceases to operate. With this the vital force is extinguished and the body decays and turns to clay. What is there to become a ghost then? If a man is without ears or eyes he lacks faculties of consciousness. Hence men who are dumb and blind are like grass or trees. But when the vital force has left a man it is a far more serious matter than simply being without ears or eyes. . . . The vital force produces man just as water becomes ice. As water freezes into ice, so the vital force coagulates to form man. When ice melts it becomes water and when a man dies he becomes spirit again. He is called spirit just as ice which has melted changes its name to water. People see that the name has changed, yet they then assert that spirit has consciousness and can assume a form and harm others, although there is no basis for this assertion.

People see ghosts which in form appear like living men. Precisely because they appear in this form, we know that they cannot be the spirits of the dead. How can we prove this? Take a sack and fill it with millet or rice. When the millet or rice has been put into it, the sack will be full and sturdy and will stand up in clear view so that people looking at it from a distance can tell that it is a sack of millet or rice. Why? Because the shape of the sack bespeaks the contents. But if the sack has a hole in it and all the millet or rice runs out, then the sack collapses in a heap and people looking from a distance can no longer see it. The spirit of man is stored up in his bodily form like the millet or rice in the sack. When he dies and his body decays, his vital force disperses like the grain running out of the sack. When the grain has run out, the sack no longer retains its shape. Then when the spirit of man has dispersed and disappeared, how could there still be a body to be seen by others? . . .

From the beginning of heaven and earth and the age of the sage rulers until now millions of people have died of old age or have been cut off in their prime. The number of men living today is nowhere near that of the dead. If men become ghosts when they die, then when we go walking we ought to see a ghost at every step. If men see ghosts when they are about to die then they ought to see millions of them crowding the hall, filling the courtyards and jamming the streets, and not just one or two of them. . . . It is the nature of Heaven and earth that, though new fires can be kindled, one cannot rekindle a fire that has burned out, and though new human beings can be born, one cannot bring back the dead. . . . Now people say that ghosts are the spirits of the dead. If this were true, then when men see them they ought to appear completely naked and not clothed in robes and sashes. Why? Because clothes have no spirits. When a man dies they all rot away along with his bodily form, so how could he put them on again? . . .

If dead men cannot become ghosts, then they also cannot have consciousness. How do we prove this? By the fact that before a man is born he has no consciousness. Before a man is born he exists in the midst of primal force (yüan-ch'i), and after he dies he returns again to this primal force. The primal force is vast and indistinct and the human force exists within it. Before a man is born he has no consciousness, so when he dies and returns to this original unconscious state how could he still have consciousness? The reason a man is intelligent and understanding is that he possesses the forces of the five virtues [humanity, righteousness, decorum, wisdom, and faith]. The reason he possesses these is that he has within him the five organs [heart, liver, stomach, lungs, and kidneys]. If these five organs are unimpaired, a man has understanding, but if they are diseased, then he becomes vague and confused and behaves like a fool or an idiot. When a man dies, the five organs rot away and the five virtues no longer have any place to reside. Both the seat and the faculty of understanding are destroyed. The body must await the vital force before it is complete, and the vital force must await the body before it can have consciousness. Nowhere is there a fire that burns all by itself. How then could there be a spirit with consciousness existing without a body? . . .

Confucius buried his mother at Fang. Later there was a heavy rain and the grave mound collapsed. When Confucius heard of this he wept bitterly and said: "The ancients did not repair graves," and he never repaired it. If the dead had consciousness then they would surely be angry that people did not repair their graves, and Confucius, realizing this, would accordingly have repaired the grave in order to please his mother's spirit. But he did not repair it. With the enlightenment of a sage he understood that the dead have no consciousness.

Yang Hsiung

Someone asks, "Don't the dragon, the tortoise, and the wild swan live very long?"

I say, "They live very long."

"Can man live very long?"

"Creatures live long because of their nature. Man does so because of his humanity (jen)." . . .

Someone asks, "If there are no immortals in the world, why do people talk about them?"

I reply, "Isn't all this talk hubbub? Because it is hubbub, it can make what is nonexistent seem to exist."

Someone then asks about the actual truth about immortals.

I say, "I shall have nothing to do with the question. Their existence or nonexistence is not something to talk about. What should be asked are questions on loyalty and filial piety."

Comment: A typical Confucian attitude toward life after death. The belief in immortals was being promoted by a religious cult worshipping the legendary Yellow Emperor of high antiquity and Lao Tzu. But to seek to live forever is contrary to the Taoist philosophy of indifference to life and death and to letting things take their own course. Therefore the belief had no place in Taoist philosophy but only in a popular cult which later assumed the name of Taoist religion.

Ch'eng I

Question: About the theory of immortals—are there such beings? *Answer:* I don't know. If you mean such things as people ascending to heaven in clear daylight, there is none. But if you mean people living in mountain forests to preserve their physical form and to imbibe energy to prolong life, then there are. It is like fire in a stove. If it is placed in the wind, it will be easily blown out. But if it is placed in a tightly closed room, it will not be easily blown out. This is in accordance with principle. *Further question:* Yang Hsiung (53 B.C.–A.D. 18) said that "the sage does not learn from immortals, for their art is not a normal one." Can sages practice the art of immortals? *Answer:* An immortal is a thief in the world. If he does not steal the secret of creation, how can he extend life forever? If sages cared to do it, Duke Chou and Confucius would have done it.

The Buddhists talk about formation, remaining in the same state, deterioration, and extinction. This indicates that they are ignorant of the Way. There are only formation and deterioration but no remaining or extinction. Take plants, for example. When they are first produced, they are already formed. As they approach the highest point of growth, they immediately began to decay. The Buddhists think that in the life of plants, they grow until they reach maturity, remain in that state for some time, and then gradually deteriorate. But nothing in the world remains in the same state. Any day added to the life of an infant means a day spent. Since when can one stay in the same state?

Taoism

Tao Te Ching
Lao Tzu

Chapter 6:

> The Valley Spirit does not die.
> This it is which is called the Mysterious Female.
> The gate of the Mysterious Female—
> This it is which is called the Root of heaven and earth.
> Lingering, lingering, [it] seems to be present;
> Its uses [can]not be exhausted.

Chapter 33:

> He who does not lose his [proper] place stays long;
> He who dies and is not gone is long-lived.

Chapter 50:

> [If] one comes out of life, one goes into death.
> The companions of life are thirteen;
> 　the companions of death are thirteen.
> The lives of men who move into the place [of] death are also thirteen.
> Why? Because they live [and strive to] live [too] heavily.
> For I heard that those who are good at preserving life
> 　walk on land, and meet no [dangers of] buffaloes, tigers;

They enter a [battling] regiment, and meet no soldierly [danger].
For in them buffaloes find nowhere to butt in,
   tigers find nowhere to claw in,
   soldiers find nowhere to knife in.
Why? Because there is no place [for] death in them.

Chapter 55:

He who thickly contains virtue
   is comparable to a newborn infant—
Wasps and adders do not sting [him];
Fierce beasts do not seize [him];
Birds of prey do not strike [him].

[He has] weak [pliable] bones, soft sinews, and a firm grip.
[He is] yet to know the male-female union, and [his] organ arouses; [this] is the
   ultimate of essence.
All day [he] shouts and is not hoarse;
   [this] is the ultimate of harmony.
To know harmony is said to be "constant";
To know the constant is said to be "clear-witted";
To benefit life is said to be "ominous";
For the mind to drive breaths is said to be "strong [straining]."

[Let] things [become] hardy, then [they become] senile;
It is called "not Tao."
Being "not Tao" will finish early.

Chapter 74:

People fear no death; why scare them with death?
Just suppose people constantly fear death, then those who do perversities we
   can arrest, and kill them—[and then] who would dare [to do perversities
   again]? [But people continue in perversities despite the constant threat of
   death; this shows that death penalty is useless. Besides,]
Constantly there is the Manager of Killing, [Nature] which kills.
To kill for the Manager of Killing, this it is which is called "hewing [woods] for
   the Great Carpenter." [Alas,]
Those who hew for the Great Carpenter seldom have not their hands
   wounded.

Chapter 75:

People starve, because those above [them] eat much taxes; this is why [they]
   starve.

People are hard to rule, because those above [them] have ado; this is why [they
   are] hard to rule.
People take death lightly, because those above [them] heavily seek life;
   this is why [they] take death lightly.
Only the ones who have nothing with which to live,
   these are wiser than to cherish life.

Chapter 76:

Birth [life] of man is soft, weak;
   his death is hard, strong.
Births [lives] of myriads of things, [such as] grass and trees, are tender and
   fragile;
   their deaths are dry and withered.
Therefore, things hard and strong are companions of death; things weak and
   tender are companions of life.
This is why soldiers, [if] strong, do not win; trees, [if] strong, suffer soliderly
   [injuries].
Things strong and big occupy low places; things tender and weak occupy high
   places.

The Chuang Tzu
(from *The Complete Works of Chuang Tzu*)

Discussion on Making All Things Equal

Tzu-Ch'i of South Wall sat leaning on his armrest, staring up at the sky
and breathing—vacant and far away, as though he'd lost his companion.
Yen Ch'eng Tzu-yu, who was standing by his side in attendance, said,
"What is this? Can you really make the body like a withered tree and the
mind like dead ashes? The man leaning on the armrest now is not the
one who leaned on it before!"

Tzu-ch'i said, "You do well to ask the question, Yen. Now I have lost
myself. Do you understand that? You hear the piping of men, but you
haven't heard the piping of earth. Or if you've heard the piping of earth,
you haven't heard the piping of Heaven!"

Tzu-yu said, "May I venture to ask what this means?"

Tzu-ch'i said, "The Great Clod belches out breath and its name is
wind. So long as it doesn't come forth, nothing happens. But when it
does, then ten thousand hollows begin crying wildly. Can't you hear
them, long drawn out? In the mountain forests that lash and sway, there
are huge trees a hundred spans around with hollows and openings like
noses, like mouths, like ears, like jugs, like cups, like mortars, like rifts,

like ruts. They roar like waves, whistle like arrows, screech, gasp, cry, wail, moan, and howl, those in the lead calling out *yeee!*, those behind calling out *yuuu!* In a gentle breeze they answer faintly, but in a full gale the chorus is gigantic. And when the fierce wind has passed on, then all the hollows are empty again. Have you never seen the tossing and trembling that goes on?"

Tzu-yu said, "By the piping of earth, then, you mean simply [the sound of] these hollows, and by the piping of man [the sound of] flutes and whistles. But may I ask about the piping of Heaven?"

Tzu-ch'i said, "Blowing on the ten thousand things in a different way, so that each can be itself—all take what they want for themselves, but who does the sounding?"

Great understanding is broad and unhurried; little understanding is cramped and busy. Great words are clear and limpid; little words are shrill and quarrelsome. In sleep, men's spirits go visiting; in waking hours, their bodies hustle. With everything they meet they become entangled. Day after day they use their minds in strife, sometimes grandiose, sometimes sly, sometimes petty. Their little fears are mean and trembly; their great fears are stunned and overwhelming. They bound off like an arrow or a crossbow pellet, certain that they are the arbiters of right and wrong. They cling to their position as though they had sworn before the gods, sure that they are holding on to victory. They fade like fall and winter—such is the way they dwindle day by day. They drown in what they do—you cannot make them turn back. They grow dark, as though sealed with seals—such are the excesses of their old age. And when their minds draw near to death, nothing can restore them to the light. . . .

Wang Ni replied, "The Perfect Man is godlike. Though the great swamps blaze, they cannot burn him; though the great rivers freeze, they cannot chill him; though swift lightning splits the hills and howling gales shake the sea, they cannot frighten him. A man like this rides the clouds and mist, straddles the sun and moon, and wanders beyond the four seas. Even life and death have no effect on him, much less the rules of profit and loss!" . . .

"How do I know that loving life is not a delusion? How do I know that in hating death I am not like a man who, having left home in his youth, has forgotten the way back?

"Lady Li was the daughter of the border guard of Ai. When she was first taken captive and brought to the state of Chin, she wept until her tears drenched the collar of her robe. But later, when she went to live in the palace of the ruler, shared his couch with him, and ate the delicious meats of his table, she wondered why she had ever wept. How do I know that the dead do not wonder why they ever longed for life?"

The Secret of Caring for Life

When Lao Tan died, Ch'in Shih went to mourn for him; but after giving three cries, he left the room.

"Weren't you a friend of the Master?" asked Lao Tzu's disciples.

"Yes."

"And you think it's all right to mourn him this way?"

"Yes," said Ch'in Shih. "At first I took him for a real man, but now I know he wasn't. A little while ago, when I went in to mourn, I found old men weeping for him as though they were weeping for a son, and young men weeping for him as though they were weeping for a mother. To have gathered a group like *that,* he must have done something to make them talk about him, though he didn't ask them to talk, or make them weep for him, though he didn't ask them to weep. This is to hide from Heaven, turn your back on the true state of affairs, and forget what you were born with. In the old days, this was called the crime of hiding from Heaven. Your master happened to come because it was his time, and he happened to leave because things follow along. If you are content with the time and willing to follow along, then grief and joy have no way to enter in. In the old days, this was called being freed from the bonds of God.

"Though the grease burns out of the torch, the fire passes on, and no one knows where it ends."

The Sign of Virtue Complete

In Lu there was a man named Wang T'ai who had had his foot cut off. He had as many followers gathered around him as Confucius.

Ch'ang Chi asked Confucius, "This Wang T'ai who's lost a foot—how does he get to divide up Lu with you, Master, and make half of it his disciples? He doesn't stand up and teach, he doesn't sit down and discuss, yet they go to him empty and come home full. Does he really have some wordless teaching, some formless way of bringing the mind to completion? What sort of man is he?"

Confucius said, "This gentleman is a sage. It's just that I've been tardy and haven't gone to see him yet. But if I go to him as my teacher, how much more should those who are not my equals! Why only the state of Lu? I'll bring the whole world along and we'll all become his followers!"

Ch'ang Chi said, "If he's lost a foot and is still superior to the Master, then how far above the common run of men he must be! A man like that—what unique way does he have of using his mind?"

Confucius said, "Life and death are great affairs, and yet they are no change to him. Though heaven and earth flop over and fall down, it is no loss to him. He sees clearly into what has no falsehood and does not shift with things. He takes it as fate that things should change, and he holds fast to the source."

"What do you mean by that?" asked Ch'ang Chi.

Confucius said, "If you look at them from the point of view of their differences, then there is liver and gall, Ch'u and Yüeh. But if you look at them from the point of view of their sameness, then the ten thousand things are all one. A man like this doesn't know what his ears or eyes should approve—he lets his mind play in the harmony of virtue. As for things, he sees them as one and does not see their loss. He regards the loss of a foot as a lump of earth thrown away."

Ch'ang Chi said, "In the way he goes about it, he uses his knowledge to get at his mind, and uses his mind to get at the constant mind. Why should things gather around *him*?"

Confucius said, "Men do not mirror themselves in running water— they mirror themselves in still water. Only what is still can still the stillness of other things. Of those that receive life from the earth, the pine and cypress alone are best—they stay as green as ever in winter or summer. Of those that receive life from Heaven, Yao and Shun alone are best—they stand at the head of the ten thousand things. Luckily they were able to order their lives, and thereby order the lives of other things. Proof that a man is holding fast to the beginning lies in the fact of his fearlessness. A brave soldier will plunge alone into the midst of nine armies. He seeks fame and can bring himself to this. How much more, then, is possible for a man who governs Heaven and earth, stores up the ten thousand things, lets the six parts of his body be only a dwelling, makes ornaments of his ears and eyes, unifies the knowledge of what he knows, and in his mind never tastes death. He will soon choose the day and ascend far off. Men may become his followers, but how could he be willing to bother himself about things?". . .

Lao Tan said, "Why don't you just make him see that life and death are the same story, that acceptable and unacceptable are on a single string? Wouldn't it be well to free him from his handcuffs and fetters?"

No-Toes said, "When Heaven has punished him, how can you set him free?"

Duke Ai of Lu said to Confucius, "In Wei there was an ugly man named Ai T'ai-T'o. But when men were around him, they thought only of him and couldn't break away, and when women saw him, they ran begging to their fathers and mothers, saying, 'I'd rather be this gentleman's concubine than another man's wife!'—there were more than ten such cases and it hasn't stopped yet. No one ever heard him take the lead—he always just chimed in with other people. He wasn't in the position of a ruler where he could save men's lives, and he had no store of provisions to fill men's bellies. On top of that, he was ugly enough to astound the whole world, chimed in but never led, and knew no more than what went on right around him. And yet men and women flocked to him. He certainly must be different from other men, I thought, and I summoned him so I could have a look. Just as they said—he was ugly enough to astound the world. But he hadn't been with me more than a month or so when I began to realize what kind of man he was, and before the year was out, I really trusted him. There was no one in the state to act as chief minister, and I wanted to hand the government over to him. He was vague about giving an answer, evasive, as though he hoped to be let off, and I was embarrassed, but in the end I turned the state over to him. Then, before I knew it, he left me and went away. I felt completely crushed, as though I'd suffered a loss and didn't have anyone left to enjoy my state with. What kind of man is he anyway?"

Confucius said, "I once went on a mission to Ch'u, and as I was going along, I saw some little pigs nursing at the body of their dead mother. After a while, they gave a start and all ran away and left her, because they could no longer see their likeness in her; she was not the same as she had been before. In loving their mother, they loved not her body but the thing that moved her body. When a man has been killed in battle and people come to bury him, he has no use for his medals. When a man has had his feet amputated, he doesn't care much about shoes. For both, the thing that is basic no longer exists. When women are selected to be consorts of the Son of Heaven, their nails are not pared and their ears are not pierced. When a man has just taken a wife, he is kept in posts outside [the palace] and is no longer sent on [dangerous] missions. If so much care is taken to keep the body whole, how much more in the case of a man whose virtue is whole? Now Ai T'ai-t'o says nothing and is trusted, accomplishes nothing and is loved, so that people want to turn over their states to him and are only afraid he won't accept. It must be that his powers are whole, though his virtue takes no form."

"What do you mean when you say his powers are whole?" asked Duke Ai.

Confucius said, "Life, death, preservation, loss, failure, success, poverty, riches, worthiness, unworthiness, slander, fame, hunger, thirst, cold, heat—these are the alternations of the world, the workings of fate. Day and night they change place before us and wisdom cannot spy out their source. Therefore, they should not be enough to destroy your harmony; they should not be allowed to enter the Spirit Storehouse. If you can harmonize and delight in them, master them and never be at a loss for joy, if you can do this day and night without break and make it be spring with everything, mingling with all and creating the moment within your own mind—this is what I call being whole in power."

"What do you mean when you say his virtue takes no form?"

"Among level things, water at rest is the most perfect, and therefore it can serve as a standard. It guards what is inside and shows no movement outside. Virtue is the establishment of perfect harmony. Though virtue takes no form, things cannot break away from it."

Some days later, Duke Ai reported his conversation to Min Tzu. "At first, when I faced south and became ruler of the realm, I tried to look after the regulation of the people and worried that they might die. I really thought I understood things perfectly. But now that I've heard the words of a Perfect Man, I'm afraid there was nothing to my understanding—I was thinking too little of my own welfare and ruining the state. Confucius and I are not subject and ruler—we are friends in virtue, that's all."

The Great and Venerable Teacher

The True Man of ancient times knew nothing of loving life, knew nothing of hating death. He emerged without delight; he went back in without a fuss. He came briskly, he went briskly, and that was all. He didn't forget where he began; he didn't try to find out where he would end. He received something and took pleasure in it; he forgot about it and handed it back again. This is what I call not using the mind to repel the Way, not using man to help out Heaven. This is what I call the True Man. . . .

Life and death are fated—constant as the succession of dark and dawn, a matter of Heaven. There are some things which man can do nothing about—all are a matter of the nature of creatures. If a man is willing to regard Heaven as a father and to love it, then how much more should he be willing to do for that which is even greater! If he is willing to regard the ruler as superior to himself and to die for him, then how much more should he be willing to do for the Truth!

When the springs dry up and the fish are left stranded on the ground, they spew each other with moisture and wet each other down with spit— but it would be much better if they could forget each other in the rivers and lakes. Instead of praising Yao and condemning Chieh, it would be better to forget both of them and transform yourself with the Way.

The Great Clod burdens me with form, labors me with life, eases me in old age, and rests me in death. So if I think well of my life, for the same reason I must think well of my death.

You hide your boat in the ravine and your fish net in the swamp and tell yourself that they will be safe. But in the middle of the night a strong man shoulders them and carries them off, and in your stupidity you don't know why it happened. You think you do right to hide little things in big ones, and yet they get away from you. But if you were to hide the world in the world, so that nothing could get away, this would be the final reality of the constancy of things.

You have had the audacity to take on human form and you are delighted. But the human form has ten thousand changes that never come to an end. Your joys, then, must be uncountable. Therefore, the sage wanders in the realm where things cannot get away from him, and all are preserved. He delights in early death; he delights in old age; he delights in the beginning; he delights in the end. If he can serve as a model for men, how much more so that which the ten thousand things are tied to and all changes alike wait upon! . . .

Nan-po Tzu-k'uei said to the Woman Crookback, "You are old in years and yet your complexion is that of a child. Why is this?"

"I have heard the Way!"

"Can the Way be learned?" asked Nan-po Tzu-k'uei.

"Goodness, how could that be? Anyway, you aren't the man to do it. Now there's Pu-liang Yi—he has the talent of a sage but not the Way of a sage, whereas I have the Way of a sage but not the talent of a sage. I thought I would try to teach him and see if I could really get anywhere near to making him a sage. It's easier to explain the Way of a sage to someone who has the talent of a sage, you know. So I began explaining and kept at him for three days, and after that he was able to put the world outside himself. When he had put the world outside himself, I kept at him for seven days more, and after that he was able to put things outside himself. When he had put things outside himself, I kept at him for nine days more, and after that he was able to put life outside himself. After he had put life outside himself, he was able to achieve the brightness of dawn, and when he had achieved the brightness of dawn, he could see his own aloneness. After he had managed to see his own aloneness, he could do away with past and present, and after he had done away with past and present, he was able to enter where there is no life and no death. That which kills life does not die; that which gives life to life does not live. This is the kind of thing it is: there's nothing it doesn't send off, nothing it doesn't welcome, nothing it doesn't destroy, nothing it doesn't complete. Its name is Peace-in-Strife. After the strife, it attains completion.". . .

Master Ssu, Master Yü, Master Li, and Master Lai were all four talking together. "Who can look upon nonbeing as his head, on life as his back, and on death as his rump?" they said. "Who knows that life and death, existence and annihilation, are all a single body? I will be his friend!"

The four men looked at each other and smiled. There was no disagreement in their hearts and so the four of them became friends.

All at once Master Yü fell ill. Master Ssu went to ask how he was. "Amazing!" said Master Yü. "The Creator is making me all crookedy like this! My back sticks up like a hunchback and my vital organs are on top of me. My chin is hidden in my navel, my shoulders are up above my head, and my pigtail points at the sky. It must be some dislocation of the yin and yang!"

Yet he seemed calm at heart and unconcerned. Dragging himself haltingly to the well, he looked at his reflection and said, "My, my! So the Creator is making me all crookedy like this!"

"Do you resent it?" asked Master Ssu.

"Why no, what would I resent? If the process continues, perhaps in time he'll transform my left arm into a rooster. In that case I'll keep watch on the night. Or perhaps in time he'll transform my right arm into a crossbow pellet and I'll shoot down an owl for roasting. Or perhaps in time he'll transform my buttocks into cartwheels. Then, with my spirit for a horse, I'll climb up and go for a ride. What need will I ever have for a carriage again?

"I received life because the time had come; I will lose it because the order of things passes on. Be content with this time and dwell in this order and then neither sorrow nor joy can touch you. In ancient times this was called the 'freeing of the bound.' There are those who cannot free themselves, because they are bound by things. But nothing can ever win against Heaven—that's the way it's always been. What would I have to resent?"

Suddenly Master Lai grew ill. Gasping and wheezing, he lay at the point of death. His wife and children gathered round in a circle and began to cry. Master Li, who had come to ask how he was, said, "Shoo! Get back! Don't disturb the process of change!"

Then he leaned against the doorway and talked to Master Lai. "How marvelous the Creator is! What is he going to make of you next? Where is he going to send you? Will he make you into a rat's liver? Will he make you into a bug's arm?"

Master Lai said, "A child, obeying his father and mother, goes wherever he is told, east or west, south or north. And the yin and yang—how much more are they to a man than father or mother! Now that they have brought me to the verge of death, if I should refuse to obey them, how perverse I would be! What fault is it of theirs? The Great Clod burdens me with form, labors me with life, eases me in old age, and rests me in death. So if I think well of my life, for the same reason I must think well of my death. When a skilled smith is casting metal, if the metal should leap up and say, 'I insist upon being made into a Mo-yeh!' he would surely regard it as very inauspicious metal indeed. Now, having had the audacity to take on human form once, if I should say, 'I don't want to be anything but a man! Nothing but a man!', the Creator would surely regard me as a most inauspicious sort of person. So now I think of heaven and earth as a great furnace, and the Creator as a skilled smith. Where could he send me that would not be all right? I will go off to sleep peacefully, and then with a start I will wake up."

Master Sang-hu, Meng-tzu Fan, and Master Ch'in-chang, three friends, said to each other, "Who can join with others without joining with others? Who can do with others without doing with others? Who can climb up to heaven and wander in the mists, roam the infinite, and forget life forever and forever?" The three men looked at each other and smiled. There was no disagreement in their hearts and so they became friends.

After some time had passed without event, Master Sang-hu died. He had not yet been buried when Confucius, hearing of his death, sent Tzu-kung to assist at the funeral. When Tzu-kung arrived, he found one of the dead man's friends weaving frames for silkworms, while the other strummed a lute. Joining their voices, they sang this song:

Ah, Sang-hu!
Ah, Sang-hu!
You have gone back to your true form
While we remain as men, O!

Tzu-kung hastened forward and said, "May I be so bold as to ask what sort of ceremony this is—singing in the very presence of the corpse?"

The two men looked at each other and laughed. "What does this man know of the meaning of ceremony?" they said.

Tzu-kung returned and reported to Confucius what had happened. "What sort of men are they anyway?" he asked. "They pay no attention to proper behavior, disregard their personal appearance and, without so much as changing the expression on their faces, sing in the very presence of the corpse! I can think of no name for them! What sort of men are they?"

"Such men as they," said Confucius, "wander beyond the realm; men like me wander within it. Beyond and within can never meet. It was stupid of me to send you to offer condolences. Even now they have joined with the Creator as men to wander in the single breath of heaven and earth. They look upon life as a swelling tumor, a protruding wen, and upon death as the draining of a sore or the bursting of a boil. To men such as these, how could there be any question of putting life first or death last? They borrow the forms of different creatures and house them in the same body. They forget liver and gall, cast aside ears and eyes, turning and revolving, ending and beginning again, unaware of where they start or finish. Idly they roam beyond the dust and dirt; they wander free and easy in the service of inaction. Why should they fret and fuss about the ceremonies of the vulgar world and make a display for the ears and eyes of the common herd?". . .

Yen Hui said to Confucius, "When Meng-sun Ts'ai's mother died, he wailed without shedding any tears, he did not grieve in his heart, and he conducted the funeral without any look of sorrow. He fell down on these three counts, and yet he is known all over the state of Lu for the excellent way he managed the funeral. Is it really possible to gain such a reputation when there are no facts to support it? I find it very peculiar indeed!"

Confucius said, "Meng-sun did all there was to do. He was advanced beyond ordinary understanding and he would have simplified things even more, but that wasn't practical. However, there is still a lot that he simplified. Meng-sun doesn't know why he lives and doesn't know why he dies. He doesn't know why he should go ahead; he doesn't know why he should fall behind. In the process of change, he has become a thing [among other things], and he is merely waiting for some other change that he doesn't yet know about. Moreover, when he is changing, how does he know that he is really changing? And when he is not changing, how does he know that he hasn't already changed? You and I, now—we are dreaming and haven't waked up yet. But in his case, though something may startle his body, it won't injure his mind; though something may alarm the house [his spirit lives in], his emotions will suffer no death. Meng-sun alone has waked up. Men wail and so he wails, too—that's the reason he acts like this.

"What's more, we go around telling each other, I do this, I do that— but how do we know that this 'I' we talk about has any 'I' to it? You dream you're a bird and soar up into the sky; you dream you're a fish and dive down in the pool. But now when you tell me about it, I don't know whether you are awake or whether you are dreaming. Running around accusing others is not as good as laughing, and enjoying a good laugh is not as good as going along with things. Be content to go along and forget about change and then you can enter the mysterious oneness of Heaven."

Heaven and Earth

Confucius said to Lao Tan, "Here's a man who works to master the Way as though he were trying to talk down an opponent, making the unacceptable acceptable, the not so, so. As the rhetoricians say, he can separate 'hard' from 'white' as clearly as though they were dangling from the eaves there. Can a man like this be called a sage?"

Lao Tan said, "A man like this is a drudging slave, a craftsman bound to his calling, wearing out his body, grieving his mind. Because the dog can catch rats, he ends up on a leash. Because of his nimbleness, the monkey is dragged down from the mountain forest. Ch'iu, I'm going to tell you something—something you could never hear for yourself and something you would never know how to speak of. People who have heads and feet but no minds and no ears—there are mobs of them. To think that beings with bodies can all go on existing along with that which is bodiless and formless—it can never happen! A man's stops and starts, his life and death, his rises and falls—none of these can he do anything about. Yet he thinks that the mastery of them lies with man! Forget things, forget Heaven, and be called a forgetter of self. The man who has forgotten self may be said to have entered Heaven."

The Way of Heaven

So it is said, for him who understands Heavenly joy, life is the working of Heaven; death is the transformation of things. In stillness, he and the yin share a single Virtue; in motion, he and the yang share a single flow. Thus he who understands Heavenly joy incurs no wrath from Heaven, no opposition from man, no entanglement from things, no blame from the spirits. So it is said, his movement is of Heaven, his stillness of earth. With his single mind in repose, he is king of the world; the spirits do not afflict him; his soul knows no weariness. His single mind reposed, the ten thousand things submit—which is to say that his emptiness and stillness reach throughout Heaven and earth and penetrate the ten thousand things. This is what is called Heavenly joy. Heavenly joy is the mind of the sage, by which he shepherds the world.

Constrained in Will

But to attain loftiness without constraining the will; to achieve moral training without benevolence and righteousness, good order without accomplishments and fame, leisure without rivers and seas, long life without Induction; to lose everything and yet possess everything, at ease in the illimitable, where all good things come to attend—this is the Way of Heaven and earth, the Virtue of the sage. So it is said, Limpidity, silence, emptiness, inaction—these are the level of Heaven and earth, the substance of the Way and its Virtue. So it is said, The sage rests; with rest comes peaceful ease, with peaceful ease comes limpidity, and where there is ease and limpidity, care and worry cannot get at him, noxious airs cannot assault him. Therefore his Virtue is complete and his spirit unimpaired.

So it is said, With the sage, his life is the working of Heaven, his death the transformation of things. In stillness, he and the yin share a single Virtue; in motion, he and the yang share a single flow. He is not the bearer of good fortune, nor the initiator of bad fortune. Roused by something outside himself, only then does he respond; pressed, only then does he move; finding he has no choice, only then does he rise up. He discards knowledge and purpose and follows along with the reasonableness of Heaven. Therefore he incurs no disaster from Heaven, no entanglement from things, no opposition from man, no blame from the spirits. His life is a floating, his death a rest. He does not ponder or scheme, does not plot for the future. A man of light, he does not shine; of good faith, he keeps no promises. He sleeps without dreaming, wakes without worry. His spirit is pure and clean, his soul never wearied. In emptiness, nonbeing, and limpidity, he joins with the Virtue of Heaven.

So it is said, Grief and happiness are perversions of Virtue; joy and anger are transgressions of the Way; love and hate are offenses against Virtue. When the mind is without care or joy, this is the height of Virtue. When it is unified and unchanging, this is the height of stillness. When it grates against nothing, this is the height of emptiness. When it has no commerce with things, this is the height of limpidity. When it rebels against nothing, this is the height of purity.

So it is said, If the body is made to labor and take no rest, it will wear out; if the spiritual essence is taxed without cessation, it will grow weary, and weariness will bring exhaustion. It is the nature of water that if it is not mixed with other things, it will be clear, and if nothing stirs it, it will be level. But if it is dammed and hemmed in and not allowed to flow, then, too, it will cease to be clear. As such, it is a symbol of Heavenly Virtue. So it is said, To be pure, clean, and mixed with nothing; still, unified, and unchanging; limpid and inactive; moving with the workings of Heaven—this is the way to care for the spirit. . . .

Perfect Happiness

People who can't get these things fret a great deal and are afraid—this is a stupid way to treat the body. People who are rich wear themselves out rushing around on business, piling up more wealth than they could ever use—this is a superficial way to treat the body. People who are eminent spend night and day scheming and wondering if they are doing right—this is a shoddy way to treat the body. Man lives his life in company with worry, and if he lives a long while, till he's dull and doddering, then he has spent that much time worrying instead of dying, a bitter lot indeed! This is a callous way to treat the body. . . .

I take inaction to be true happiness, but ordinary people think it is a bitter thing. I say: perfect happiness knows no happiness, perfect praise knows no praise. The world can't decide what is right and what is wrong. And yet inaction can decide this. Perfect happiness, keeping alive—only inaction gets you close to this!

Let me try putting it this way. The inaction of Heaven is its purity, the inaction of earth is its peace. So the two inactions combine and all things are transformed and brought to birth. Wonderfully, mysteriously, there is no place they come out of. Mysteriously, wonderfully, they have no sign. Each thing minds its business and all grow up out of inaction. So I say, Heaven and earth do nothing and there is nothing that is not done. Among men, who can get hold of this inaction?

Chuang Tzu's wife died. When Hui Tzu went to convey his condolences, he found Chuang Tzu sitting with his legs sprawled out, pounding on a tub and singing. "You lived with her, she brought up your children and grew old," said Hui Tzu. "It should be enough simply not to weep at her death. But pounding on a tub and singing—this is going too far, isn't it?"

Chuang Tzu said, "You're wrong. When she first died, do you think I didn't grieve like anyone else? But I looked back to her beginning and the time before she was born. Not only the time before she was born, but the time before she had a body. Not only the time before she had a body, but the time before she had a spirit. In the midst of the jumble of wonder and mystery a change took place and she had a spirit. Another change and she had a body. Another change and she was born. Now there's been another change and she's dead. It's just like the progression of the four seasons, spring, summer, fall, winter.

"Now she's going to lie down peacefully in a vast room. If I were to follow after her bawling and sobbing, it would show that I don't understand anything about fate. So I stopped."

Uncle Lack-Limb and Uncle Lame-Gait were seeing the sights at Dark Lord Hill and the wastes of K'un-lun, the place where the Yellow Emperor rested. Suddenly a willow sprouted out of Uncle Lame-Gait's left elbow. He looked very startled and seemed to be annoyed.

"Do you resent it?" said Uncle Lack-Limb.

"No—what is there to resent?" said Uncle-Lame-Gait. "To live is to borrow. And if we borrow to live, then life must be a pile of trash. Life and death are day and night. You and I came to watch the process of change, and now change has caught up with me. Why would I have anything to resent?"

When Chuang Tzu went to Ch'u, he saw an old skull, all dry and parched. He poked it with his carriage whip and then asked, "Sir, were you greedy for life and forgetful of reason, and so came to this? Was your state overthrown and did you bow beneath the ax, and so came to this? Did you do some evil deed and were you ashamed to bring disgrace upon your parents and family, and so came to this? Was it through the pangs of cold and hunger that you came to this? Or did your springs and autumns pile up until they brought you to this?"

When he had finished speaking, he dragged the skull over and, using it for a pillow, lay down to sleep.

In the middle of the night, the skull came to him in a dream and said, "You chatter like rhetorician and all your words betray the entanglements of a living man. The dead know nothing of these! Would you like to hear a lecture on the dead?"

"Indeed," said Chuang Tzu.

The skull said, "Among the dead there are no rulers above, no subjects below, and no chores of the four seasons. With nothing to do, our springs and autumns are as endless as heaven and earth. A king facing south on his throne could have no more happiness than this!"

Chuang Tzu couldn't believe this and said, "If I got the Arbiter of Fate to give you a body again, make you some bones and flesh, return you to your parents and family and your old home and friends, you would want that, wouldn't you?"

The skull frowned severely, wrinkling up its brow. "Why would I throw away more happiness than that of a king on a throne and take on the troubles of a human being again?" it said. . . .

Lieh Tzu was on a trip and was eating by the roadside when he saw a hundred-year-old skull. Pulling away the weeds and pointing his finger, he said, "Only you and I know that you have never died and you have never lived. Are you really unhappy? Am I really enjoying myself?"

The Mountain Tree

The Master from south of the Market said, "Make few your needs, lessen your desires, and then you may get along even without rations. You will ford the rivers and drift out upon the sea. Gaze all you may— you cannot see its farther shore; journey on and on—you will never find where it ends. Those who came to see you off will all turn back from the shore and go home, while you move ever farther into the distance.

"He who possesses men will know hardship; he who is possessed by men will know care. Therefore Yao neither possessed men nor allowed himself to be possessed by them. So I ask you to rid yourself of hardship, to cast off your cares, and to wander alone with the Way to the Land of Great Silence.

"If a man, having lashed two hulls together, is crossing a river, and an empty boat happens along and bumps into him; no matter how hot-tempered the man may be, he will not get angry. But if there should be someone in the other boat, then he will shout out to haul this way or veer that. If his first shout is unheeded, he will shout again, and if that is not heard, he will shout a third time, this time with a torrent of curses following. In the first instance, he wasn't angry; now in the second he is. Earlier he faced emptiness, now he faces occupancy. If a man could succeed in making himself empty, and in that way wander through the world, then who could do him harm?". . .

Confucius was besieged between Ch'en and Ts'ai, and for seven days he ate no cooked food. T'ai-kung Jen went to offer his sympathy. "It looks as if you're going to die," he said.

"It does indeed."

"Do you hate the thought of dying?"

"I certainly do!"

Jen said, "Then let me try telling you about a way to keep from dying. In the eastern sea there is a bird and its name is Listless. It flutters and flounces but seems to be quite helpless. It must be boosted and pulled before it can get into the air, pushed and shoved before it can get back to its nest. It never dares to be the first to advance, never dares to be the last to retreat. At feeding time, it never ventures to take the first bite, but picks only at the leftovers. So, when it flies in file, it never gets pushed aside, nor do other creatures such as men ever do it any harm. In this way it escapes disaster."

Knowledge Wandered North

"Life is the companion of death, death is the beginning of life. Who understands their workings? Man's life is a coming-together of breath. If it comes together, there is life; if it scatters, there is death. And if life and death are companions to each other, then what is there for us to be anxious about? . . .

Shun asked Ch'eng, "Is it possible to gain possession of the Way?"

"You don't even have possession of your own body—how could you possibly gain possession of the Way!"

"If I don't have possession of my own body, then who does?" said Shun.

"It is a form lent you by Heaven and earth. You do not have possession of life—it is a harmony lent by Heaven and earth. You do not have possession of your inborn nature and fate—they are contingencies lent by Heaven and earth. You do not have possession of your sons and grandsons—they are castoff skins lent by Heaven and earth. So it is best to walk without knowing where you are going, stay home without knowing what you are guarding, eat without knowing what you are tasting. All is the work of the Powerful Yang in the world. How then could it be possible to gain possession of anything?". . .

"Here is a man of the Middle Kingdom, neither yin nor yang, living between heaven and earth. For a brief time only, he will be a man, and then he will return to the Ancestor. Look at him from the standpoint of the Source and his life is a mere gathering together of breath. And whether he dies young or lives to a great old age, the two fates will scarcely differ—a matter of a few moments, you might say. How, then, is it worth deciding that Yao is good and Chieh is bad? . . .

"Man's life between heaven and earth is like the passing of a white colt glimpsed through a crack in the wall—whoosh!—and that's the end. Overflowing, starting forth, there is nothing that does not come out; gliding away, slipping into silence, there is nothing that does not go back in. Having been transformed, things find themselves alive; another transformation and they are dead. Living things grieve over it, mankind mourns. But it is like the untying of the Heaven-lent bow-bag, the unloading of the Heaven-lent satchel—a yielding, a mild mutation, and the soul and spirit are on their way, the body following after, on at last to the Great Return.

"The formless moves to the realm of form; the formed moves back to the realm of formlessness. This all men alike understand. But it is not something to be reached by striving. The common run of men all alike debate how to reach it. But those who have reached it do not debate, and those who debate have not reached it. Those who peer with bright eyes will never catch sight of it. Eloquence is not as good as silence. The Way cannot be heard; to listen for it is not as good as plugging up your ears. This is called the Great Acquisition." . . .

"Why don't you try wandering with me to the Palace of Not-Even-Anything—identity and concord will be the basis of our discussions and they will never come to an end, never reach exhaustion. Why not join with me in inaction, in tranquil quietude, in hushed purity, in harmony and leisure? Already my will is vacant and blank. I go nowhere and don't know how far I've gotten. I go and come and don't know where to stop. I've already been there and back, and I don't know when the journey is done. I ramble and relax in unbordered vastness; Great Knowledge enters in, and I don't know where it will ever end.

"That which treats things as things is not limited by things. Things have their limits—the so-called limits of things. The unlimited moves to the realm of limits; the limited moves to the unlimited realm. We speak of the filling and emptying, the withering and decay of things. [The Way] makes them full and empty without itself filling or emptying; it makes them wither and decay without itself withering or decaying. It establishes root and branch but knows no root and branch itself; it determines when to store up or scatter but knows no storing or scattering itself."

Ah Ho-kan and Shen Nung were studying together under Old Lung Chi. Shen Nung sat leaning on his armrest, the door shut, taking his daily nap, when at midday Ah Ho-kan threw open the door, entered and announced, "Old Lung is dead!"

Shen Nung, still leaning on the armrest, reached for his staff and jumped to his feet. Then he dropped the staff with a clatter and began to laugh, saying, "My Heaven-sent Master—he knew how cramped and mean, how arrogant and willful I am, and so he abandoned me and died. My Master went off and died without ever giving me any wild words to open up my mind!"

Yen Kang-tiao, hearing of the incident, said, "He who embodies the Way has all the gentlemen of the world flocking to him. As far as the Way goes, Old Lung hadn't gotten hold of a piece as big as the tip of an autumn hair, hadn't found his way into one ten-thousandth of it—but even *he* knew enough to keep his wild words stored away and to die with them unspoken. How much more so, then, in the case of a man who embodies the Way! Look for it but it has no form, listen but it has no voice. Those who discourse upon it with other men speak of it as dark and mysterious. The Way that is discoursed upon is not the Way at all!". . .

Jan Ch'iu asked Confucius, "Is it possible to know anything about the time before Heaven and earth existed?"

Confucius said, "It is—the past is the present."

Jan Ch'iu, failing to receive any further answer, retired. The following day he went to see Confucius again and said, "Yesterday I asked if it were possible to know anything about the time before Heaven and earth existed, and you, Master, replied, 'It is—the past is the present.' Yesterday that seemed quite clear to me, but today it seems very obscure. May I venture to ask what this means?"

Confucius said, "Yesterday it was clear because your spirit took the lead in receiving my words. Today, if it seems obscure, it is because you are searching for it with something other than spirit, are you not? There is no past and no present, no beginning and no end. Sons and grandsons existed before sons and grandsons existed—may we make such a statement?"

Jan Ch'iu had not replied when Confucius said "Stop!—don't answer!

Do not use life to give life to death. Do not use death to bring death to life. Do life and death depend upon each other? Both have that in them which makes them a single body. There is that which was born before Heaven and earth, but is it a thing? That which treats things as things is not a thing. Things that come forth can never precede all other things, because there were already things existing then; and before that, too, there were already things existing—so on without end. The sage's love of mankind, which never comes to an end, is modeled on this principle."

Yen Yüan said to Confucius, "Master, I have heard you say that there should be no going after anything, no welcoming anything. May I venture to ask how one may wander in such realms?"

Confucius said, "The men of old changed on the outside but not on the inside. The men of today change on the inside but not on the outside. He who changes along with things is identical with him who does not change. Where is there change? Where is there no change? Where is there any friction with others? Never will he treat others with arrogance. But Hsi-wei had his park, the Yellow Emperor his garden, Shun his palace, T'ang and Wu their halls. And among gentlemen there were those like the Confucians and Mo-ists who became 'teachers.' As a result, people began using their 'rights' and 'wrongs' to push each other around. And how much worse are the men of today!

"The sage lives with things but does no harm to them, and he who does no harm to things cannot in turn be harmed by them. Only he who does no harm is qualified to join with other men in 'going after' or 'welcoming.'

"The mountains and forests, the hills and fields fill us with overflowing delight and we are joyful. Our joy has not ended when grief comes trailing it. We have no way to bar the arrival of grief and joy, no way to prevent them from departing. Alas, the men of this world are no more than travelers, stopping now at this inn, now at that, all of them run by 'things.' They know the things they happen to encounter, but not those that they have never encountered. They know how to do the things they can do, but they can't do the things they don't know how to do. Not to know, not to be able to do—from these mankind can never escape. And yet there are those who struggle to escape from the inescapable—can you help but pity them? Perfect speech is the abandonment of speech; perfect action is the abandonment of action. To be limited to understanding only what is understood—this is shallow indeed!"

Keng-Sang Ch'u

The Way permeates all things. Their dividedness is their completeness, their completeness is their impairment. What is hateful about this state of dividedness is that men take their dividedness and seek to supplement it; and what is hateful about attempts to supplement it is that they are a mere supplementation of what men already have. So they go forth and forget to return—they act as though they had seen a ghost. They go forth and claim to have gotten something—what they have gotten is the thing called death. They are wiped out and choked off— already a kind of ghost themselves. Only when that which has form learns to imitate the formless will it find serenity.

It comes out from no source, it goes back in through no aperture. It has reality yet no place where it resides; it has duration yet no beginning or end. Something emerges, though through no aperture—this refers to the fact that it has reality. It has reality yet there is no place where it resides—this refers to the dimension of space. It has duration but no beginning or end—this refers to the dimension of time. There is life, there is death, there is a coming out, there is a going back in—yet in the coming out and going back its form is never seen. This is called the Heavenly Gate. The Heavenly Gate is nonbeing. The ten thousand things come forth from nonbeing. Being cannot create being out of being; inevitably it must come forth from nonbeing. Nonbeing is absolute nonbeing, and it is here that the sage hides himself.

The understanding of the men of ancient times went a long way. How far did it go? To the point where some of them believed that things have never existed—so far, to the end, where nothing can be added. Those at the next stage thought that things exist. They looked upon life as a loss, upon death as a return—thus they had already entered the state of dividedness. Those at the next stage said, "In the beginning there was nonbeing. Later there was life, and when there was life suddenly there was death. We look upon nonbeing as the head, on life as the body, on death as the rump. Who knows that being and nonbeing, life and death are a single way? I will be his friend!"

Tse-Yang

"Before they are born, things cannot decline to be born; already dead, they cannot refuse to go. Death and life are not far apart, though the principle that underlies them cannot be seen. 'Nothing does it,' 'something makes it like this'—these are speculations born out of doubt. I look for the roots of the past, but they extend back and back without end. I search for the termination of the future, but it never stops coming at me. Without end, without stop, it is the absence of words, which shares the same principle with things themselves. But 'nothing does it,' 'something makes it like this'—these are the commencement of words and they begin and end along with things.

"The Way cannot be thought of as being, nor can it be thought of as nonbeing. In calling it the Way we are only adopting a temporary expedient. 'Nothing does it,' 'something makes it like this'—these occupy a mere corner of the realm of things. What connection could they have with the Great Method? If you talk in a worthy manner, you can talk all day long and all of it will pertain to the Way. But if you talk in an unworthy manner, you can talk all day long and all of it will pertain to mere things. The perfection of the Way and things—neither words nor silence are worthy of expressing it. Not to talk, not to be silent—this is the highest form of debate."

Lieh Yü-K'ou

Someone sent gifts to Chuang Tzu with an invitation to office. Chuang Tzu replied to the messenger in these words: "Have you ever seen a sacrificial ox? They deck him out in embroidery and trimmings, gorge him on grass and beanstalks. But when at last they lead him off into the great ancestral temple, then, although he might wish he could become a lonely calf once more, is it possible?"

When Chuang Tzu was about to die, his disciples expressed a desire to give him a sumptuous burial. Chuang Tzu said, "I will have heaven and earth for my coffin and coffin shell, the sun and moon for my pair of jade discs, the stars and constellations for my pearls and beads, and the ten thousand things for my parting gifts. The furnishings for my funeral are already prepared—what is there to add?"

"But we're afraid the crows and kites will eat you, Master!" said his disciples.

Chuang Tzu said, "Above ground I'll be eaten by crows and kites, below ground I'll be eaten by mole crickets and ants. Wouldn't it be rather bigoted to deprive one group in order to supply the other?

"If you use unfairness to achieve fairness, your fairness will be unfair. If you use a lack of proof to establish proofs, your proofs will be proofless. The bright-eyed man is no more than the servant of things, but the man of spirit knows how to find real proofs. The bright-eyed is no match for the man of spirit—from long ago this has been the case. Yet the fool trusts to what he can see and immerses himself in the human. All his accomplishments are beside the point—pitiful, isn't it!"

The World

Blank, boundless, and without form; transforming, changing, never constant: are we dead? are we alive? do we stand side by side with Heaven and earth? do we move in the company of spiritual brightness? absent-minded, where are we going? forgetful, where are we headed for? The ten thousand things ranged all around us, not one of them is worthy to be singled out as our destination—there were those in ancient times who believed that the "art of the Way" lay in these things. Chuang Chou heard of their views and delighted in them. He expounded them in odd and outlandish terms, in brash and bombastic language, in unbound and unbordered phrases, abandoning himself to the times without partisanship, not looking at things from one angle only. He believed that the world was drowned in turbidness and that it was impossible to address it in sober language. So he used "goblet words" to pour out endless changes, "repeated words" to give a ring of truth, and "imputed words" to impart greater breath. He came and went alone with the pure spirit of Heaven and earth, yet he did not view the ten thousand things with arrogant eyes. He did not scold over "right" and "wrong," but lived with the age and its vulgarity. Though his writings are a string of queer beads and baubles, they roll and rattle and do no one any harm. Though his words seem to be at sixes and sevens, yet among the sham and waggery there are things worth observing, for they are crammed with truths that never come to an end.

Above he wandered with the Creator, below he made friends with those who have gotten outside of life and death, who know nothing of beginning or end. As for the Source, his grasp of it was broad, expansive, and penetrating; profound, liberal, and unimpeded. As for the Ancestor, he may be said to have tuned and accommodated himself to it and to have risen on it to the greatest heights. Nevertheless, in responding to change and expounding on the world of things, he set forth principles that will never cease to be valid, an approach that can never be shuffled off. Veiled and arcane, he is one who has never been completely comprehended.

The Hindu Tradition

(from *The Thirteen Principal Upanishads*)

Brihad-Āraṇyaka Upanishad

Verily, that [sun] which gives forth heat is the Aśva-medha. The year is its embodiment (*ātman*).

This [earthly] fire is the *arka*. The worlds are its embodiments. These are two, the *arka* sacrificial fire and the Aśva-medha sacrifice. Yet again they are one divinity, even Death. He [who knows this] wards off repeated death (punarmṛtyu), death obtains him not, death becomes his body (ātman), he becomes one of these deities.

Fifth Brāhmaṇa

> 1.When the Father produced by intellect
>   And austerity seven kinds of food,
>   One of his [foods] was common to all,
>   Of two he let the gods partake,
>   Three he made for himself,
>   One he bestowed upon the animals.
>   On this [food] everything depends,
>   Both what breathes and what does not.
>   How is it that these do not perish
>   When they are being eaten all the time?
>   He who knows this imperishableness—
>   He eats food with his mouth (pratīka),
>   He goes to the gods,
>   He lives on strength.

Thus the verses.

2. 'When the Father produced by intellect and austerity seven kinds of food'—truly by intellect and austerity the Father did produce them.

'One of his [foods] was common to all.' That of his which is common to all is the food that is eaten here. He who worships that, is not turned from evil, for it is mixed [i.e. common, not selected].

'Of two he let the gods partake.' They are the huta (fire-sacrifice) and the prahuta (offering). For this reason one sacrifices and offers to the gods. People also say that these two are the new-moon and the full-moon sacrifices. Therefore one should not offer sacrifice [merely] to secure a wish.

'One he bestowed upon the animals'—that is milk, for at first both men and animals live upon milk. Therefore they either make a new-born babe lick butter or put it to the breast. Likewise they call a new-born calf 'one that does not eat grass.'

'On this [food] everything depends, both what breathes and what does not'—for upon milk everything depends, both what breathes and what does not. This that people say, 'By offering with milk for a year one escapes repeated death (punarmṛtyu)'—one should know that this is not so, since on the very day that he makes the offering he who knows escapes repeated death, for he offers all his food to the gods.

'How is it that these do not perish when they are being eaten all the time?' Verily, the Person is imperishableness, for he produces this food again and again.

'He who knows this imperishableness'—verily, a person is imperishableness, for by continuous meditation he produces this food as his work. Should he not do this, all the food would perish.

'He eats food with his mouth (pratīka).' The pratīka is the mouth. So he eats food with his mouth.

'He goes to the gods, he lives on strength'—this is praise.

Bṛihad-Āraṇyaka Upanishad

17. Now next, the Transmission.— When a man thinks he is about to depart, he says to his son: 'Thou art holy knowledge. Thou art sacrifice. Thou art the world.' The son replies: 'I am holy knowledge. I am sacrifice. I am the world.' Verily, whatever has been learned [from the Vedas], the sum of all this is expressed by the word 'knowledge' (brahma). Verily, whatever sacrifices have been made, the sum of them all is expressed by the word 'sacrifice.' Whatever worlds there are, they are all comprehended under the word 'world.' So great, verily, is this all.

'Being thus the all, let him assist me from this world,' thus [the father considers]. Therefore they call 'world-procuring' a son who has been instructed. Therefore they instruct him.

When one who has this knowledge departs from this world, he enters into his son with these vital breaths [i.e. faculties: Speech, Mind, and Breath]. Whatever wrong has been done by him, his son frees him from it all. Therefore he is called a son (putra). By his son a father stands firm in this world. Then into him [who has made over to his son his mortal breaths] enter those divine immortal breaths.

18. From the earth and from the fire the divine Speech enters him. Verily, that is the divine Speech whereby whatever one says comes to be.

19. Out of the sky and out of the sun the divine Mind enters him. Verily, that is the divine Mind whereby one becomes blissful and sorrows not.

20. Out of the water and out of the moon the divine Breath enters him. Verily, that is the divine Breath which, whether moving or not moving, is not perturbed, nor injured.

He who knows this becomes the Self of all beings. As is that divinity [i.e. Prajāpati], so is he. As all beings favor that divinity, so to him who knows this all beings show favor. Whatever sufferings creatures endure, these remain with them. Only good goes to him. Evil, verily, does not go to the gods.

Breath, the unfailing power in a person: like the
unwearying world-breath, wind

21. Now next, a Consideration of the Activities.—

Prajāpati created the active functions *(karma)*. They, when they had been created, strove with one another. 'I am going to speak,' the voice began. 'I am going to see,' said the eye. 'I am going to hear,' said the ear. So spake the other functions, each according to his function. Death, appearing as weariness, laid hold and took possession of them; and, taking possession of them, Death checked them. Therefore the voice becomes weary, the eye becomes weary, the ear becomes weary. But Death did not take possession of him who was the middle breath. They sought to know him. They said: 'Verily, he is the best of us, since whether moving or not moving, he is not perturbed, nor perishes. Come, let us all become a form of him.' Of him, indeed, they became a form. Therefore they are named 'vital breaths' after him. In whatever family there is a man who has this knowledge, they call that family after him. Whoever strives with one who knows this, dries up and finally dies.— So much with reference to the self.

22. Now with reference to the divinities.—

'Verily, I am going to blaze,' began the Fire. 'I am going to give forth heat,' said the Sun. 'I am going to shine,' said the Moon. So said the other divinities, each according to his divine nature. As Breath holds the central position among the vital breaths [or functions], so Wind among these divinities; for the other divinities have their decline, but not Wind. The Wind is that divinity which never goes to rest.

23. There is this verse on the subject:—

From whom the sun rises
And in whom it sets—

in truth, from Breath it rises, and in Breath it sets—

Him the gods made law *(dharma);*
He only today and tomorrow will be.

Verily, what those [functions] undertook of old, even that they accomplish today. Therefore one should practise but one activity. He should breathe in and breathe out, wishing, 'May not the evil one, Death, get me.' And the observance which he practises he should desire to fulfil to the end. Thereby he wins complete union with that divinity [i.e. Breath] and residence in the same world.

Bṛihad-Āraṇyaka Upanishad

10. 'Yājñavalkya,' said he, 'since everything here is food for death, who, pray, is that divinity for whom death is food?'

'Death, verily, is a fire. It is the food of water *(āpas)*. He wards off *(apa-jayati)* repeated death [who knows this].'

11. 'Yājñavalkya,' said he, 'when a man dies, do the breaths go out of him, or no?'

'No,' said Yājñavalkya. 'They are gathered together right there. He swells up. He is inflated. The dead man lies inflated.'

12. 'Yājñavalkya,' said he, 'when a man dies, what does not leave him?'

'The name. Endless, verily, is the name. Endless are the All-gods. An endless world he wins thereby.'

13. 'Yājñavalkya,' said he, 'when the voice of a dead man goes into fire, his breath into wind, his eye into the sun, his mind into the moon, his hearing into the quarters of heaven, his body into the earth, his soul *(ātman)* into space, the hairs of his head into plants, the hairs of his body into trees, and his blood and semen are placed in water, what then becomes of this person *(puruṣa)?*'

'Artabhāga, my dear, take my hand. We two only will know of this. This is not for us two [to speak of] in public.'

The two went away and deliberated. What they said was *karma* (action). What they praised was *karma*. Verily, one becomes good by good action, bad by bad action.

Thereupon Jāratkārava Ārtabhāga held his peace.

Fourth Brāhmaṇa

1. When this self comes to weakness and to confusedness of mind, as it were, then the breaths gather around him. He takes to himself those particles of energy and descends into the heart. When the person in the eye turns away, back [to the sun], then one becomes non-knowing of forms.

2. "He is becoming one," they say; "he does not see." "He is becoming one," they say; "he does not smell." "He is becoming one," they say; "he does not taste." "He is becoming one," they say; "he does not speak." "He is becoming one," they say; "he does not hear." "He is becoming one," they say; "he does not think." "He is becoming one," they say; "he does not touch." "He is becoming one," they say; "he does not know." The point of his heart becomes lighted up. By that light the self departs, either by the eye, or by the head, or by other bodily parts. After him, as he goes out, the life *(prāṇa)* goes out. After the life, as it goes out, all the breaths *(prāṇa)* go out. He becomes one with intelligence. What has intelligence departs with him. His knowledge and his works and his former intelligence [i.e. instinct] lay hold of him.

Fifth Brāhmaṇa

Now Kahola Kaushītakeya questioned him, 'Yājñavalkya,' said he, 'explain to me him who is just the Brahma present and not beyond our ken, him who is the Soul in all things.'

'He is your soul, which is in all things.'

'Which one, O Yājñavalkya, is in all things?'

'He who passes beyond hunger and thirst, beyond sorrow and delusion, beyond old age and death—Brahmans who know such a Soul overcome desire for sons, desire for wealth, desire for worlds, and live the life of mendicants. For desire for sons is desire for wealth, and desire for wealth is desire for worlds, for both these are merely desires. Therefore let a Brahman become disgusted with learning and desire to live as a child. When he has become disgusted both with the state of childhood and with learning, then he becomes an ascetic *(muni)*. When he has become disgusted both with the non-ascetic state and with the ascetic state, then he becomes a Brahman.'

'By what means would he become a Brahman?'

'By what means by which he does become such a one. Aught else than this Soul *(Ātman)* is wretched.'

Thereupon Kahola Kaushītakeya held his peace.

12. Man *(puruṣa)*, verily, is a sacrificial fire, O Gautama. The open mouth, verily, is its fuel; breath *(prāṇa)*, the smoke; speech, the flame; the eye, the coals; the ear, the sparks. In this fire the gods offer food. From this oblation semen arises.

13. Woman, verily, is a sacrificial fire, O Gautama. The sexual organ, in truth, is its fuel; the hairs, the smoke; the vulva, the flame; when one inserts, the coals; the feelings of pleasure, the sparks. In this oblation the gods offer semen. From this oblation a person *(puruṣa)* arises.

He lives as long as he lives. Then when he dies, [14] then they carry him to the fire. His fire, in truth, becomes the fire, fuel, the fuel; smoke, the smoke; flame, the flame; coals, the coals; sparks, the sparks. In this fire the gods offer a person *(puruṣa)*. From this oblation the man arises, having the color of light.

15. Those who knew this, and those too who in the forest truly worship *(upāsate)* faith *(śraddhā)*, pass into the flame [of the cremation-fire]; from the flame, into the day; from the day, into the half month of the waxing moon; from the half month of the waxing moon, into the six months during which the sun moves northward; from these months, into the world of the gods *(deva-loka);* from the world of the gods, into the sun; from the sun, into the lightning-fire. A Person *(puruṣa)*

consisting of mind *(mānasa)* goes to those regions of lightning and conducts them to the Brahma-worlds. In those Brahma-worlds they dwell for long extents. Of these there is no return.

16. But they who by sacrificial offering, charity, and austerity conquer the worlds, pass into the smoke [of the cremation-fire]; from the smoke, into the night; from the night, into the half month of the waning moon; from the half month of the waning moon, into the six months during which the sun moves southward; from those months, into the world of the fathers; from the world of the fathers, into the moon. Reaching the moon, they become food. There the gods—as they say to King Soma, "Increase! Decrease!"—even so feed upon them there. When that passes away for them, then they pass forth into this space; from space, into air; from air, into rain; from rain, into the earth. On reaching the earth they become food. Again they are offered in the fire of man. Thence they are born in the fire of woman. Rising up into the world, they cycle round again thus.

But those who know not these two ways, become crawling and flying insects and whatever there is here that bites.'

Tenth Brāhmaṇa

The course to Brahma after death

Verily, when a person *(puruṣa)* departs from this world he goes to the wind. It opens out there for him like the hole of a chariot-wheel. Through it he mounts higher.

He goes to the sun. It opens out there for him like the hole of a drum. Through it he mounts higher.

He goes to the moon. It opens out for him there like the hole of a kettle-drum. Through it he mounts higher.

He goes to the world that is without heat, without cold. Therein he dwells eternal years.

Chāndogya Upanishad

5. Now, whether they perform the cremation obsequies in the case of such a person or not, they [i.e. the dead] pass over into a flame; from a flame, into the day; from the day, into the half-month of the waxing moon; from the half-month of the waxing moon, into the six months during which the sun moves northwards; from the months, into the year; from the year, into the sun; from the sun, into the moon; from the moon, into lightning. Then there is a Person *(puruṣa)* who is non-human *(a-mānava)*.

6. He leads them on to Brahma. This is the way to the gods, the way

to Brahma. They who proceed by it return not to the human condition here—yea, they return not!'

When a person here is deceasing, my dear, his voice goes into his mind; his mind, into his breath; his breath, into heat; the heat, into the highest divinity. (7) That which is the finest essence—[7] this whole world has that as its soul. That is Reality (satya). That is Ātman (Soul). That art thou, Śvetaketu.'

'Do you, sir, cause me to understand even more.'

'So be it, my dear,' said he.

Chāndogya Upanishad

4. Now, when one thus becomes reduced to weakness, those sitting around say: 'Do you know me?' 'Do you know me?' As long as he has not departed from this body, he knows them.

5. But when he thus departs from this body, then he ascends upward with these very rays of the sun. With the thought of *Om*, verily, he passes up. As quickly as one could direct his mind to it, he comes to the sun. That, verily, indeed, is the world-door, an entrance for knowers, a stopping for non-knowers.

6. As to this there is the following verse:—

There are a hundred and one channels of the heart.
One of these passes up to the crown of the head.
Going up by it, one goes to immortality.
The others are for departing in various directions.

Kaushitaki Upanishad

The testing at the moon; thence either return to earth or further progress

2. Then he said: 'Those who, verily, depart from this world—to the moon, in truth, they all go. During the earlier half it thrives on their breathing spirits (prāna); with the latter half it causes them to be reproduced. This, verily, is the door of the heavenly world—that is, the moon. Whoever answers it, him it lets go further. But whoever answers it not, him, having become rain, it rains down here. Either as a worm, or as a moth, or as a fish, or as a bird, or as a lion, or as a wild boar, or as a snake, or as a tiger, or as a person, or as some other in this or that condition, he is born again here according to his deeds (karman), according to his knowledge.

His identity with life and immortality

2. Then he said: 'I am the breathing spirit (prāna), the intelligential self (prajñātman). As such (tam), reverence me as life (āyus), as immor-

tality. Life is the breathing spirit. The breathing spirit, verily, is life. The breathing spirit, indeed, is immortality. For, as long as the breathing spirit remains in this body, so long is there life. For indeed, with the breathing spirit in this world one obtains immortality; with intelligence, true conception *(saṁkalpa)*.

So he who reverences me as life, as immortality, reaches the full term of life in this world; he obtains immortality, indestructibility *(akṣiti)* in the heavenly world *(svarga-loka)*.'

Iśa Upanishad

Becoming and destruction a fundamental duality

14. Becoming *(sambhūti)* and destruction *(vināśa)*—
He who this pair conjointly (saha) knows,
With destruction passing over death,
With becoming wins the immortal.

A dying person's prayer

15. With a golden vessel
The Real's face is covered o'er.
That do thou, O Pūshan, uncover
For one whose law is the Real to see.

16. O Nourisher *(pūṣan)*, the sole Seer *(ekarṣi)*, O Controller *(yama)*, O Sun *(sūrya)*, offspring of Prajāpati, spread forth thy rays! Gather thy brilliance *(tejas)!* What is thy fairest form—that of thee I see. He who is yonder, yonder Person *(puruṣa)*—I myself am he!

17. [My] breath *(vāyu)* to the immortal wind *(anila)!* This body then ends in ashes! *Om!*

O Purpose *(kratu)*, remember! The deed *(kṛta)* remember!
O Purpose, remember! The deed remember!

General prayer of petition and adoration

18. O Agni, by a goodly path to prosperity *(rai)* lead us,
Thou god who knowest all the ways!
Keep far from us crooked-going sin *(enas)!*
Most ample expression of adoration to thee would we render!

Muṇḍaka Upanishad

In tranquil union with the Soul of all is liberation from death and from all distinctions of individuality

5. Attaining Him, the seers *(ṛṣi)* who are satisfied with knowledge,

Who are perfected souls *(kṛtātman)*, from passion free *(vītarāga)*, tranquil—
Attaining Him who is the universally omnipresent, those wise,
Devout souls *(yukātman)* into the All itself do enter.

6. They who have ascertained the meaning of the Vedānta-knowledge,
Ascetics *(yati)* with natures purified through the application of renunciation *(saṁnyāsa-yoga)*—
They in the Brahma-worlds at the end of time
Are all liberated beyond death.

7. Gone are the fifteen parts according to their station,
Even all the sense-organs *(deva)* in their corresponding divinities!
One's deeds *(karman)* and the self that consists of understanding *(vijñāna-maya ātman)*—
All become unified in the supreme Imperishable.

8. As the flowing rivers in the ocean
Disappear, quitting name and form,
So the knower, being liberated from name and form,
Goes unto the Heavenly Person, higher than the high.

Śvetāśvatara Upanishad

She [i.e. Nature, Prakṛiti], too, is unborn, who is connected with the enjoyer and objects of enjoyment.
Now, the soul *(ātman)* is infinite, universal, inactive.
When one finds out this triad, that is Brahma.

10. What is perishable, is Primary Matter *(pradhāna)*. What is immortal and imperishable, is Hara (the 'Bearer,' the soul).
Over both the perishable and the soul the One God *(deva)* rules.
By meditation upon Him, by union with Him, and by entering into His being
More and more, there is finally cessation from every illusion *(māyā-nivṛtti)*.

11. By knowing God *(deva)* there is a falling off of all fetters;
With distresses destroyed, there is cessation of birth and death.
By meditating upon Him there is a third stage at the dissolution of the body,
Even universal lordship; being absolute *(kevala)*, his desire is satisfied.

12. That Eternal should be known as present in the self *(ātmasaṁstha)*.
Truly there is nothing higher than that to be known.
When one recognizes the enjoyer, the object of enjoyment, and the universal Actuator,
All has been said. This is the threefold Brahma.

2.12 When the fivefold quality of Yoga has been produced,
Arising from earth, water, fire, air, and space,
No sickness, no old age, no death has he
Who has obtained a body made out of the fire of Yoga.

13. Lightness, healthiness, steadiness,
Clearness of countenance and pleasantness of voice,
Sweetness of odor, and scanty excretions—
These, they say, are the first stage in the progress of Yoga.
Knowing the One Supreme Person overcomes death.

7. Higher than this is Brahma. The Supreme, the Great,
Hidden in all things, body by body,
The One embracer of the universe—
By knowing Him as Lord (*īs*) men become immortal.

8. I know this mighty Person (Purusha)
Of the color of the sun, beyond darkness.
Only by knowing Him does one pass over death.
There is no other path for going there.

9. Than whom there is naught else higher,
Than whom there is naught smaller, naught greater,
The One stands like a tree established in heaven.
By Him, the Person, this whole world is filled.

10. That which is beyond this world
Is without form and without ill.
They who know That, become immortal;
But others go only to sorrow.

15. He indeed is the protector of the world in time,
The overlord of all, hidden in all things,
With whom the seers of Brahma and the divinities are joined in union.
By knowing Him thus, one cuts the cords of death.

16. By knowing as kindly (*śiva*) Him who is hidden in all things,
Exceedingly fine, like the cream that is finer than butter,
The One embracer of the universe—
By knowing God (*deva*) one is released from all fetters.

17. That God, the All-worker, the Great Soul (*mahātman*),
Ever seated in the heart of creatures,
Is framed by the heart, by the thought, by the mind—
They who know That, become immortal.

18. When there is no darkness, then there is no day or night,
Nor being, nor non-being, only the Kindly One (*śiva*) alone.
That is the Imperishable. 'That [is the] choicest [splendor] of Savitṛi (the Sun).'

And from that was primeval Intelligence *(prajñā)* created.

19. Not above, not across,
   Nor in the middle has one grasped Him.
   There is no likeness of Him
   Whose name is Great Glory *(mahad yaśas).*

20. His form is not to be beheld.
   No one soever sees Him with the eye.
   They who thus know Him with heart and mind
   As abiding in the heart, become immortal.

Praśna Upanishad

The departure of a Person's Life

3.7. Now, rising upward through one of these [channels], the up-breath *(udāna)* leads in consequence of good [work] *(puṇya)* to the good world; in consequence of evil *(pāpa)*, to the evil world; in consequence of both, to the world of men.

[e and f] Its cosmic and personal relations

8. The sun, verily, rises externally as life; for it is that which helps the life-breath in the eye. The divinity which is in the earth supports a person's out-breath *(apāna)*. What is between [the sun and the earth], namely space *(ākāśa)*, is the equalizing breath *(samāna)*. The wind (Vāyu) is the diffused breath *(vyāna)*.

9. Heat *(tejas)*, verily, is the up-breath *(udāna)*. Therefore one whose heat has ceased goes to rebirth, with his senses *(indriya)* sunk in mind *(manas)*.

One's thinking determines life and destiny

10. Whatever is one's thinking *(citta)*, therewith he enters into life *(prāṇa)*. His life joined with his heat, together with the self *(ātman)*, leads to whatever world has been fashioned [in thought].

6.5. As these flowing rivers that tend toward the ocean, on reaching the ocean, disappear, their name and form *(nāma-rūpa)* are destroyed, and it is called simply "the ocean"—even so of this spectator these sixteen parts that tend toward the Person, on reaching the Person, disappear, their name and form are destroyed, and it is called simply "the Person." That one continues without parts, immortal! As to that there is this verse:—

6. Whereon the parts rest firm
   Like the spokes on the hub of a wheel—
   Him I know as the Person to be known!
   So let death disturb you not!'

The Buddhist Tradition

(from *Buddhism in Translations*)

Translated from the Visuddhi-Magga (chap. xviii.)

Just as the word "chariot" is but a mode of expression for axle, wheels, chariot-body, pole, and other constituent members, placed in a certain relation to each other, but when we come to examine the members one by one, we discover that in the absolute sense there is no chariot; and just as the word "house" is but a mode of expression for wood and other constituents of a house, surrounding space in a certain relation, but in the absolute sense there is no house; and just as the word "fist" is but a mode of expression for the fingers, the thumb, etc., in a certain relation; and the word "lute" for the body of the lute, strings, etc.; "army" for elephants, horses, etc.; "city" for fortifications, houses, gates, etc.; "tree" for trunk, branches, foliage, etc., in a certain relation, but when we come to examine the parts one by one, we discover that in the absolute sense there is no tree; in exactly the same way the words "living entity" and "Ego" are but a mode of expression for the presence of the five attachment groups, but when we come to examine the elements of being one by one, we discover that in the absolute sense there is no living entity there to form a basis for such figments as "I am," or "I"; in other words, that in the absolute sense there is only name and form. The insight of him who perceives this is called knowledge of the truth.

He, however, who abandons this knowledge of the truth and believes in a living entity must assume either that this living entity will perish or that it will not perish. If he assume that it will not perish, he falls into the heresy of the persistence of existences; or if he assume that it will perish, he falls into that of the annihilation of existences. And why do I say so? Because, just as sour cream has milk as its antecedent, so nothing here exists but what has its own antecedents. To say, "The living entity persists," is to fall short of the truth; to say, "It is annihilated," is to outrun the truth. Therefore has The Blessed One said:—

"There are two heresies, O priests, which possess both gods and men, by which some fall short of the truth, and some outrun the truth; but the intelligent know the truth.

Translated from the Visuddhi-Magga (chap. xvi.).

Therefore has it been said as follows:—

"Misery only doth exist, none miserable.
No doer is there; naught save the deed is found.

Nirvana is, but not the man who seeks it.
The Path exists, but not the traveler on it."

Translated from the Milindapañha (40).

"Bhante Nāgasena," said the king, "is a person when just born that person himself, or is he some one else?"

"He is neither that person," said the elder, "nor is he some one else."

"Give an illustration."

"What do you say to this, your majesty? When you were a young, tender, weakly infant lying on your back, was that your present grown-up self?"

"Nay, verily, bhante. The young, tender, weakly infant lying on its back was one person, and my present grown-up self is another person."

"It is as if, your majesty, new milk were to change in process of time into sour cream, and from sour cream into fresh butter, and from fresh butter into clarified butter. And if any one, your majesty, were to say that the sour cream, the fresh butter, and the clarified butter were each of them the very milk itself—now would he say well, if he were to say so?"

"Nay, verily, bhante. They came into being through connection with that milk."

"In exactly the same way, your majesty, do the elements of being join one another in serial succession: one element perishes, another arises, succeeding each other as it were instantaneously.

The Round of Existence
Translated from the Milindapañha (77).

"Bhante Nāgasena," said the king, "when you say 'round of existence,' what is that?"

"Your majesty, to be born here and die here, to die here and be born elsewhere, to be born there and die there, to die there and be born elsewhere,—this, your majesty, is the round of existence."

"Give an illustration."

"It is as if, your majesty, a man were to eat a ripe mango, and plant the seed; and from that a large mango-tree were to spring and bear fruit; and then the man were to eat a ripe mango from that tree also and plant the seed; and from that seed also a large mango-tree were to spring and bear fruit; thus of these trees there is no end discernible. In exactly the same way, your majesty, to be born here and die here, to die here and be born elsewhere, to be born there and die there, to die there and be born elsewhere, this, your majesty, is the round of existence."

"You are an able man, bhante Nāgasena."

Cause of Rebirth
Translated from the Milindapañha (32).

"Bhante Nāgasena," said the king, "are there any who die without being born into another existence?"

"Some are born into another existence," said the elder, "and some are not born into another existence."

"Who is born into another existence, and who is not born into another existence?"

"Your majesty, he that still has the corruptions is born into another existence; he that no longer has the corruptions is not born into another existence."

"But will you, bhante, be born into another existence?"

"Your majesty, if there shall be in me any attachment, I shall be born into another existence; if there shall be in me no attachment, I shall not be born into another existence."

"You are an able man, bhante Nāgasena."

Is This to Be My Last Existence?
Translated from the Milindapañha (41).

"Bhante Nāgasena," said the king, "does a man know when he is not to be born into another existence?"

"Assuredly, your majesty, a man knows when he is not to be born into another existence."

"Bhante, how does he know it?"

"He knows it from the cessation of all cause or reason for being born into another existence."

"Give an illustration."

"It is as if, your majesty, a house-holding farmer were to plow and sow and fill his granary; and then were neither to plow nor sow, and were to use the grain previously stored up, or give it away, or do with it however else might suit him: your majesty, would this house-holding farmer know that his granary would not become filled up again?"

"Assuredly, bhante, would he know it."

"How would he know it?"

"He would know it from the cessation of all cause or reason for the filling up of the granary."

"In exactly the same way, your majesty, a man knows when he is not to be born into another existence, from the cessation of all cause or reason for being born into another existence."

"You are an able man, bhante Nāgasena."

Different Kinds of Death
Translated from the Visuddhi-Magga (chap. viii.).

By death is meant the cutting off of the vitality comprised in any one existence. Now the death of the saint, which consists in the annihilation of the misery of rebirth; incessant death, which is the incessant breaking up of the constituents of being; and death in popular parlance, as when it is said, "The tree is dead, the iron is dead,"—none of these is meant here. But what is meant here is twofold, either natural death, or untimely death.

Natural death occurs either by the exhaustion of merit, or by the exhaustion of the natural term of life, or by the exhaustion of both.

Untimely death occurs by karma cutting off karma.

Death by the exhaustion of merit is death which supervenes when the karma which caused conception has ripened to a termination, although the dependence for continuing the series constituting the term of life be not exhausted. Death by the exhaustion of the natural term of life occurs when the span of life, the nutritive powers, etc., proper to any given grade of existence, come to an end,—in the present race of men on the exhaustion of their natural term of life at the age of only one hundred years.

Untimely death is death like that of Dusī Māra, or of king Kalābu and others, who had their series cut off by karma that carried them off on the spot, or like that of such persons as have their series cut off by a bloody death brought upon them by the karma of a previous existence.

Death's Messengers.
Translated from the Aṅguttara-Nikāya (iii. 35).

Death has three messengers, O priests. And what are the three?

Suppose, O priests, one does evil with his body, does evil with his voice, does evil with his mind. Having done evil with his body, done evil with his voice, and done evil with his mind, he arrives after the dissolution of the body, after death, at a place of punishment, a place of suffering, perdition, hell. Then, O priests, the guardians of hell seize him by the arms at every point, and they show him to Yama, the ruler of the dead, saying,

"Sire, this man did not do his duty to his friends, to his parents, to the monks, or to the Brahmans, nor did he honor his elders among his kinsfolk. Let your majesty inflict punishment upon him."

Then, O priests, king Yama questions, sounds, and addresses him touching the first of death's messengers.

"O man! Did you not see the first of death's messengers visibly appear among men?"

He replies, "Lord, I did not."

Then, O priests, king Yama says to him, "O man! Did you not see among men a woman or a man, eighty or ninety or a hundred years of age, decrepit, crooked as the curved rafter or a gable roof, bowed down, leaning on a staff, trembling as he walked, miserable, with youth long fled, broken-toothed, gray-haired and nearly bald, tottering, with wrinkled brow, and blotched with freckles?"

He replies, "Lord, I did."

Then, O priests, king Yama says to him, "O man! Did it not occur to you, being a person of mature intelligence and years, 'I also am subject to old age, and in no way exempt. Come now! I will act nobly with body, voice, and mind'?"

He replies, "Lord, I could not. Lord, I did not think."

Then, O priests, king Yama says to him, "O man! Through thoughtlessness you failed to act nobly with body, voice, and mind. Verily, it shall be done unto you, O man, in accordance with your thoughtlessness. And it was not your mother who did this wickedness, nor was it your father, nor your brother, nor your sister, nor your friends and companions, nor your relatives and kinsfolk, nor the deities, nor the monks and Brahmans; but it was you yourself who did this wickedness, and you alone shall feel its consequences."

Then, O priests, the guardians of hell take him feet up, head down, and throw him into a heated iron kettle that is blazing, flaming, and glowing. There he cooks and sizzles. And while he there cooks and sizzles, he goes once upwards, once downwards, and once sideways. There he experiences grievous, severe, sharp, and bitter pains; but he does not die so long as that wickedness is unexhausted.

Now this, O priests, that I tell you, I did not get from any one else, be he monk or Brahman; but, O priests, what I by myself, unassisted, have known, and seen, and learnt, that I tell you.

> All they who thoughtless are, nor heed,
> What time death's messengers appear,
> Must long the pangs of suffering feel
> In some base body habiting.
> But all those good and holy men,
> What time they see death's messengers,
> Behave not thoughtless, but give heed
> To what the Noble Doctrine says;

And in attachment frighted see
Of birth and death the fertile source,
And from attachment free themselves,
Thus birth and death extinguishing,
Secure and happy ones are they,
Released from all this fleeting show;
Exempted from all sin and fear,
All misery have they overcome.

The Attainment of the Paths
Translated from the Visuddhi-Magga (chap. xxi.).

"Behold how empty is the world,
Mogharāja! In thoughtfulness
Let one remove belief in self
And pass beyond the realm of death.
The king of death can never find
The man who thus the world beholds."

When in the course of his application of the Three Characteristics the ascetic has thus considered the constituents of being in the light of their emptiness, he abandons all fear and joy in regard to them, and becomes indifferent and neutral, and does not deem them as "I" or "mine," like a man who has given up his wife.

Just as a man might have a wife beloved, delightful, and charming, from whom he could not bear to be separated for a moment, and on whom he excessively doted. If he then were to see that woman standing or sitting in company with another man, and talking and joking with him, he would be angry and displeased, and experience bitter grief. But if subsequently he were to discover that she had been guilty of a fault, he would lose all desire for her and let her go, and no longer look on her as "mine." From that time on, whenever he might see her engaged with any one else, he would not be angry or grieved, but simply indifferent and neutral. In exactly the same way the ascetic by grasping the constituents of being with the reflective insight becomes desirous of being released from them, and perceiving none of them worthy of being deemed "I" or "mine," he abandons all fear and joy in regard to them, and becomes indifferent and neutral. When he has learnt and perceived this, his mind draws in, contracts, and shrinks away from the three modes of existence, the four species of being, the five destinies in rebirth, the seven stages of consciousness, the nine grades of being, and does not spread out, and only indifference or disgust abides. . . .

"Moreover, deliverance has three starting-points for escape from the world: the consideration of the beginnings and endings of the constituents of being for the thoughts to spring to the unconditioned; the agitating of the mind concerning the constituents of being for the thoughts to spring to the desireless; the consideration of all the elements of being as not an Ego for the thoughts to spring to the empty. These are the three starting-points of deliverance for escape from the world."

Here *the beginnings and endings*—the beginnings and endings in the springing up and disappearance of things. For the insight into transitoriness, by coming to the conclusion, "The constituents of being did not exist before they sprang up," determines beginnings; and by observing their destiny, and coming to the conclusion, "They continue no more after they have disappeared, but vanish right then," determines endings.

The *agitating of the mind*—the agitating of the thoughts. For by insight into the misery of the constituents of being the thoughts are agitated.

The *consideration of all the elements of being as not an Ego*—considering them as not an "I" or "mine."

Accordingly these three propositions are to be understood as spoken concerning the insight into transitoriness etc. Therefore was it thereafter said in answer to a question.

"To one who considers them in the light of their transitoriness the constituents of being seem perishable. To one who considers them in the light of their misery they seem frightful. To one who considers them in the light of their want of an Ego they seem empty."

But how many are the deliverances of which these insights are the starting-points? There are three: the unconditioned, the desireless, and the empty. For it has been said as follows:

"He who considers them [the constituents of being] in the light of their transitoriness abounds in faith and obtains the unconditioned deliverance; he who considers them in the light of their misery abounds in tranquillity and obtains the desireless deliverance; he who considers them in the light of their want of an Ego abounds in knowledge and obtains the empty deliverance."

Here *the unconditioned deliverance* is the Noble Path realized by meditation on Nirvana in its unconditioned aspect. For the Noble Path is unconditioned from having sprung out of the unconditioned, and it is a deliverance from being free from the corruptions. In the same way the Noble Path when realized by meditation on Nirvana in its desireless aspect is to be understood as *desireless;* when realized by meditation on Nirvana in its empty aspect as *empty.*

Nirvana to Be Attained at Death
Translated from the Visuddhi-Magga (chap. xxii.).

Just as, however, a man displeased with the flowers, fruit, etc. of a tree, will pierce it on each of its four sides with the poisonous thorn called the maṇḍu-thorn, and then that tree, when its earth-extracted juices and its sap have become exhausted by the application of that poison, will arrive at a state of inability to bear fruit and not be able to reproduce itself; in exactly the same way a youth of good family, displeased with the existence of the groups, will, like the man who applied poison to the tree on each of its four sides, begin to apply the meditation of the Four Paths to the series of his groups. And then the series of his groups, when the rebirth-causing corruptions have become exhausted by the application of the poison of the Four Paths, resolves itself into such bodily and other kinds of karma as constitute barren action; and arriving at a state of not being liable to be reborn in the future, and unable to reproduce itself in the next existence, by the cessation of the last consciousness becomes like a fire without fuel, and passes into Nirvana without attachment.

The Attainment of Nirvana by Godhika.
Translated from the Dhammapada, and from
Buddhaghosa's Commentary to stanza 57.

This venerable man, while dwelling at Black Rock on the slopes of Isigili, being vigilant, austere, and strenuous, attained release for his mind in ecstatic meditation, and then through the power of a disease which beset him, the trance was broken up. A second time, a third time, up to the sixth time was his trance broken up.

At the seventh time, he thought,

"Six times has my trance been broken up, and doubtful is the fate of those who fail in trance. This time I will resort to the knife."

And taking a razor for shaving the hair, he lay down on a couch in order to cut his windpipe. . . .

At that moment the Slayer, the Wicked One, had become a pillar of smoke, as it were, or a bunch of darkness; and wondering to himself, "Where can it have fixed itself?" was searching in all directions for the elder's rebirth-consciousness. . . .

"Where has Godhika gone? Though I search upwards and downwards, and to all the points and intermediate points of the compass, I do not meet him."

Then said The Teacher to him,

"Always in meditation found
That brave, strong man his best delight;
Each day and night he practised it,
And recked not, cared not, for his life.

"Thus vanquished he Namuci's host;
No more to rebirth he returns.
Lo! Godhika uproots desire,
And, dying, has Nirvana gained."

The Demon solely mortified,
Down from his side let fall the lute;
And in a sore, dejected mood,
He straightway disappeared from sight.

Translated from the Visuddhi-Magga (chap. xxiii.).

What is the trance of cessation?

It is the stoppage of all mentality by a gradual cessation. . . . A priest who is desirous of entering on cessation will take his breakfast, wash carefully his hands and his feet, and seat him cross-legged on a well-strewn seat in some retired spot, with body erect, and contemplative faculty active. He then enters the first trance, and rising from it obtains insight into the transitoriness, misery, and lack of an Ego of the constituents of being.

This insight, however, is threefold: the insight into the constituents of being, the insight belonging to the attainment of the Fruits, and the insight belonging to the trance of cessation. . . .

In regard to this elder, tradition has it that he went for alms to the village where lived his mother, a lay devotee. The lay devotee gave him some rice-gruel and asked him to sit down in a reception-hall. The elder sat down and entered on cessation. While he was sitting there, the reception-hall took fire, and all the other priests took up the several mats on which they had been sitting, and fled away. The inhabitants of the village came together, and seeing the elder, cried out, "The lazy monk! the lazy monk!" The fire blazed up in the grass, bamboo, sticks of wood, etc., completely surrounding the elder. The people brought water in pitchers and put it out, removed the ashes and made the ground neat again, and scattering flowers stood worshiping him. The elder rose from his trance, when the fixed term had elapsed, and seeing the people gazing at him, sprang up into the air, and went to the island Piyañgu. This is the protection of less intimate belongings.

Articles, however, which are intimately joined to the person of the priest, such as his tunic, his upper garment, or the seat on which he may be sitting, do not need any special resolve. The trance is sufficient to protect them, as in the case of the venerable Sañjīva. For it has been said as follows:

"The concentration of the venerable Sañjīva possesses magical power; the concentration of the venerable Sāriputta possesses magical power." . . .

Limitation of time—limitation of the time of life. For this priest should be skilful respecting the limitation of time. He should not enter this trance without first reflecting whether his span of life is to last seven days longer or not. For if he were to enter this trance without perceiving that his vital powers were to break up within the seven-day limit, his trance of cessation would not be able to ward off death, and as death cannot take place during cessation, he would have to rise from the midst of his trance. Therefore he must enter it only after having made the above reflection. For it has been said that it is permissible to neglect the other reflections, but not this one.

When he has thus entered the realm of nothingness, and risen from it and performed these preliminary duties, he enters the realm of neither perception nor yet non-perception; and having passed beyond one or two thoughts, he stops thinking and reaches cessation. But why do I say that beyond two thoughts the thoughts cease? Because of the priest's progress in cessation. For the priest's progress in gradual cessation consists in an ascent through the eight attainments by the simultaneous use of both the quiescence and insight methods, and does not result from the trance of the realm of neither perception nor yet non-perception alone. Thus it is because of the priest's progress in cessation that beyond two thoughts the thoughts cease. . . .

What is the difference between a dead man and one who has entered this trance? This matter also is treated of in this discourse. As it is said:

"Brother, of the man who has died and become a corpse, bodily karma has ceased and become quieted, vocal karma has ceased and become quieted, mental karma has ceased and become quieted, vitality has become exhausted, natural heat has subsided, and the senses have broken up. Of the priest who has entered on the cessation of perception and sensation, bodily karma has ceased and become quieted, vocal karma has ceased and become quieted, mental karma has ceased and become quieted, but vitality has not become exhausted, natural heat has not subsided, and the senses have not broken up." . . .

The Buddha in Nirvana

This brief passage from the Questions of King Menander *illustrates the Theravāda conception of Nirvāna. It is not total annihilation, but at the same*

time it involves the complete disintegration of the phenomenal personality—a
paradox which cannot be explained in words.

"Reverend Nāgasena," said the King, "does the Buddha still exist?"

"Yes, your Majesty, he does."

"Then is it possible to point out the Buddha as being here or there?"

"The Lord has passed completely away in Nirvāna, so that nothing is
left which could lead to the formation of another being. And so he
cannot be pointed out as being here or there."

"Give me an illustration."

"What would your Majesty say—if a great fire were blazing, would it
be possible to point to a flame which had gone out and say that it was
here or there?"

"No, your Reverence, the flame is extinguished, it can't be detected."

"In just the same way, your Majesty, the Lord has passed away in
Nirvāna. . . . He can only be pointed out in the body of his doctrine, for
it was he who taught it."

"Very good, Reverend Nāgasena!"

[From *Milindapañha* (Trenckner, ed.), p. 73]

Swampland Flowers
Ta Hui

When his old acquaintance ascended the throne in 1163 as Emperor
Hsiao Tsung, Ta Hui came under imperial protection. It was this
emperor who bestowed the title "Ch'an Master of Great Wisdom" from
which the name Ta Hui comes, and who caused Ta Hui's words to be
included in the Great Canon a few years after his death.

It was 1163, on the ninth day of the eighth month, after showing signs
of illness, when Ta Hui told the congregation of monks, nuns, and
laypeople, "Tomorrow I'm going." Towards the pre-dawn hours, after
he'd written his last bequest and a letter to the emperor, the monk who
was his attendant asked Ta Hui for a verse. In a serious voice Ta Hui
said, "Without a verse, I couldn't die." He took up the brush and wrote:

Birth is thus
Death is thus
Verse or no verse
What's the fuss?

Then he let go of the writing brush and passed on. He had lived seventy-five years, fifty-eight in Ch'an. Records of his teachings were assembled by his disciples. . . .

To Liu Li-kao

Facing Death

You report that the last day of your life has already arrived. You should contemplate just like this in your daily activities—then the mind of worldly affliction will naturally come to an end. When the mind of affliction has come to an end, then the next day as before, early spring is still chilly. An ancient worthy said, "If you want to know the meaning of Buddha-nature, you must observe times and seasons, causes and conditions." This melting away of the mind of affliction is the time and season of Old Yellow Face (Buddha) appearing in the world and achieving buddhahood, the time and season of his sitting upon the Diamond Seat (of enlightenment), vanquishing armies of delusive demons, turning the Wheel of the Dharma, delivering sentient beings, and entering *nirvana*. It's no different from the time you've called "the last day of your life." To get here, just contemplate like this: This contemplation is called correct contemplation; contemplation different from this is called wrong contemplation. If you don't distinguish incorrect from correct, you won't avoid shifting and changing following after the times and seasons of others. If you want to get so you aren't following times and seasons, simply abandon it at once. Put it down where it can't be put down.

Don't take these words either. As before, it's just you, layman—there's no other man besides.

The Tibetan Tradition

Tibetan Book of the Dead(1)

The Great Liberation Through Hearing in the Bardo

Bardo means gap; it is not only the interval of suspension after we die but also suspension in the living situation; death happens in the living situation as well. The bardo experience is part of our basic psychological make-up. There are all kinds of bardo experiences happening to us all the time, experiences of paranoia and uncertainty in everyday life; it is like not being sure of our ground, not knowing quite what we have asked for or what we are getting into. So this book is not only a message for those who are going to die and those who are already dead, but it is also a message for those who are already born; birth and death apply to everybody constantly, at this very moment.

The bardo experience can be seen in terms of the six realms of existence that we go through, the six realms of our psychological states.

The Main Verses of the Six Bardos

> Now when the bardo of birth is dawning upon me,
> I will abandon laziness for which life has no time,
> enter the undistracted path of study, reflection and meditation,
> making projections and mind the path, and realise the three kāyas;
> now that I have once attained a human body,
> there is no time on the path for the mind to wander.
>
> Now when the bardo of dreams is dawning upon me,
> I will abandon the corpse-like sleep of careless ignorance,
> and let my thoughts enter their natural state without distraction;
> controlling and transforming dreams in luminosity,
> I will not sleep like any animal
> but unify completely sleep and practice.
>
> Now when the bardo of samādhi-meditation dawns upon me,
> I will abandon the crowd of distractions and confusions,
> and rest in the boundless state without grasping or disturbance;
> firm in the two practices: visualisation and complete;
> at this time of meditation, one-pointed, free from activity,
> I will not fall into the power of confused emotions.
>
> Now when the bardo of the moment before death dawns upon me,
> I will abandon all grasping, yearning and attachment,
> enter undistracted into clear awareness of the teaching,
> and eject my consciousness into the space of unborn mind;
> as I leave this compound body of flesh and blood
> I will know it to be a transitory illusion.
>
> Now when the bardo of dharmatā dawns upon me,
> I will abandon all thoughts of fear and terror,
> I will recognise whatever appears as my projection
> and know it to be a vision of the bardo;
> now that I have reached this crucial point,
> I will not fear the peaceful and wrathful ones, my own projections.

Now when the bardo of becoming dawns upon me,
I will concentrate my mind one-pointedly,
and strive to prolong the results of good karma,
close the womb-entrance and think of resistance;
this is the time when perseverance and pure thought are needed,
abandon jealousy, and meditate on the guru with his consort.

With mind far off, not thinking of death's coming,
performing these meaningless activities,
returning empty-handed now would be complete confusion;
the need is recognition, holy dharma,
so why not practise dharma at this very moment?
From the mouths of siddhas come these words:
If you do not keep your guru's teaching in your heart
will you not become your own deceiver?

Tibetan Book of the Dead (2)

Even though thou dost not experience pleasure, or pain, but only indifference, keep thine intellect in the undistracted state of the [meditation upon the] Great Symbol, without thinking that thou art meditating.[1] This is of vast importance.

O nobly-born, at that time, at bridge-heads, in temples, by *stūpas* of eight kinds,[2] thou wilt rest a little while, but thou wilt not be able to remain there very long, for thine intellect hath been separated from thine [earth-plane] body.[3] Because of this inability to loiter, thou oft-times wilt feel perturbed and vexed and panic-stricken. At times, thy Knower will be dim; at times, fleeting and incoherent. Thereupon this thought will occur to thee, 'Alas! I am dead! What shall I do?' and because of such thought the Knower will become saddened and the heart chilled, and thou wilt experience infinite misery of sorrow.[4] Since thou canst not rest in any one place, and feel impelled to go on, think not of various things, but allow the intellect to abide in its own [unmodified] state.

As to food, only that which hath been dedicated to thee can be partaken of by thee, and no other food.[5] As to friends at this time, there will be no certainty.[6]

These are the indications of the wandering about on the *Sidpa Bardo* of the mental-body. At the time, happiness and misery will depend upon *karma*.

Thou wilt see thine own home, the attendants, relatives, and the corpse, and think, 'Now I am dead! What shall I do?' and being oppressed with intense sorrow, the thought will occur to thee, 'O what would I not give to possess a body!' And so thinking, thou wilt be wandering hither and thither seeking a body.

Even though thou couldst enter thy dead body nine times over—owing to the long interval which thou hast passed in the *Chönyid Bardo*—it will have been frozen if in winter, been decomposed if in summer, or, otherwise, thy relatives will have cremated it, or interred it, or thrown it into the water, or given it to the birds and beasts of prey.[7] Wherefore finding no place for thyself to enter into, thou wilt be dissatisfied and have the sensation of being squeezed into cracks and crevices amidst rocks and boulders.[8] The experiencing of this sort of misery occurs in the Intermediate State when seeking rebirth. Even though thou seekest a body, thou wilt gain nothing but trouble. Put aside the desire for a body; and permit thy mind to abide in the state of resignation, and act so as to abide therein.

By thus being set face to face, one obtaineth liberation from the *Bardo*.

1. Text: *bsgom-med-yengs-med* (pron. *yom-med-yeng-med*) = 'non-meditation + non-distraction'; referring to a state of mental concentration in which no thought of meditation itself is allowed to intrude. This is the state of *Samādhi*. If one thinks one is meditating, the thought alone inhibits the meditation; hence the warning to the deceased.

2. This refers to the eight purposes for which a *stūpa* (or pagoda) is built. Two such instances may be cited in elucidation: (1) *rnam-rgyal-mchod-rten* (pron. *ram-gyal-chōd-ten*): *mchod-rten* (or *chorten* = *stūpa*) is here translatable as 'object of worship', and *rnam-rgyal* as 'victory'; hence this sort of pagoda is one for marking a victory, i.e. a monument; (2) *myang-hdas-mchod-rten* (pron. *nyang-day-chöd-ten*) refers to a *stūpa* used as a monument for marking the spot where a saint or sage died, or the place of burial of the urn containing such a one's ashes. Other pagodas are purely symbolical structures erected—as Christian crosses are—as objects of worship or veneration. In Ceylon many *stūpas* are erected solely to enshrine sacred books or reliques. The great *stūpas* of North-west India, near Peshawar and at Taxila, lately opened, contained bone-reliques and other objects. Two of them contained authentic bits of the bones of the Buddha.

3. Like a person travelling alone at night along a highway, having his attention arrested by prominent landmarks, great isolated trees, houses, bridge-heads, temples, *stūpas*, and so on, the dead, in their own way, have similar experiences when earth-wandering. They are attracted, by *karmic* propensities, to familiar haunts in the human world, but being possessed of a mental or desire body cannot remain long at any one place. As our text explains, they are driven hither and thither by the winds of *karmic* desires—like a feather before a gale.

4. It should be remembered here that all the terrifying phenomena and the unhappiness are entirely *karmic*. Had the deceased been developed spiritually, his *Bardo* existence would have been peaceful and happy from the first, and he would not have wandered down so far as this. The *Bardo Thödol* is concerned chiefly with the normal individual, and not with highly developed human beings whom death sets free into Reality.

5. Like fairies and spirits of the dead according to Celtic belief, or the daemons of ancient Greek belief, the dwellers in the *Bardo* are said to live on invisible ethereal essences, which they extract either from food offered to them on the human plane or else from the general store-house of nature. In *The Six Doctrines*, already referred to above (p. 162^2), there is this reference to the inhabitants of the *Bardo:* 'They live on odours [or the spiritual essences of material things].'

6. Friends may or may not exist in the Intermediate State, as on earth; but even if they do, they are powerless to counteract any bad *karma* of the deceased. He must follow his own path, as marked out by *karma*.

7. All known forms of disposal of a corpse are practised in Tibet, including mummification. (See pp. 25–8.)

8. This symbolizes the getting into undesirable wombs, such as those of human beings of animal-like nature.

CHAPTER 3
Stoics, Epicureans, Christians, and Skeptics

The time frame with which this chapter is concerned extends from about 300 B.C. (Epicurus) to the beginning of the seventeenth century (Montaigne). Obviously much more has been written about death in these 2,000 years of Western philosophy than can be included in this chapter. We have undertaken, therefore, to present the four major perspectives on death that arose in this era, and to offer some representative samples of the philosophers who developed these views. The four major "schools" of thought about death during these years share the quality of being a philosophical way of life. They are: 1) Stoicism, 2) Epicureanism, 3) Christianity and 4) skepticism. Each, in its own way, teaches us that death is an inevitable part of life, that life moves inexorably towards death, and that we are a long way from truly understanding this universal phenomenon.

1. The Stoics (Epictetus and Marcus Aurelius) remind us constantly that death must come to all men. Death is part of the natural order of things; we cannot control death, therefore we ought not to concern ourselves about it. The laws of nature are immutable; we struggle against necessity only to lose our happiness. But our attitude, *our reaction to death,* is within our control. Only when we live in accordance with the universal laws of nature, that is, only when we will our behavior and attitude to follow necessity, can we reach the state of "apatheia," or spiritual well-being, the highest good in life. The quietism of the stoic results from a deep understanding of the inevitability of death.

Epictetus (c. 50–c. 130) was born a slave, gained his freedom sometime after the death of Nero in 68, and died in exile from Rome as master of a thriving school of philosophy. His influence on Stoicism is enormous, embodying the Stoic sentiments of indifference and forbearance in the face of death. The selections reprinted below are from *Epictetus,* translated by W. A. Oldfather.

Marcus Aurelius Antoninus (121–180) was a statesman and Emperor of Rome. His only extant work, *The Meditations,* has been praised as the greatest ethical product of Ancient Rome. It consists of twelve books describing his philosophic beliefs with great clarity of thought and style. His views on death are similar to those of Epictetus', which he frequently quoted. The selection reprinted below is translated by George Long, from *The Meditations of Marcus Aurelius.*

2. The Epicureans (Epicurus and Lucretius) founded an ethical way of life which emphasized pleasure and the absence of pain as man's highest good. This physical and mental well-being was called "ataraxia," and was possible only when one realizes that death is the cessation of experience. Through the study of natural philosophy we must train our minds to accept the fact that death means nothing to us. We cannot feel death, we cannot live death, and we cannot experience death, therefore we ought not to fear death.

Epicurus (341 B.C.–270 B.C.) was born on the Greek island of Samos, but he and his followers eventually settled in Athens where they established a community called the Garden. There Epicurus developed and taught a philosophy which incorporated much of earlier pre-Socratic thought. Epicurus borrowed from Democritus that theory of physics which stated that death was part of a cycle of disintegration. All human functions, including death, are the results of atomic processes. Therefore, Epicurus tells us, "death means nothing to us, since every good and every evil lies in sensation; but death is the privation of sensation." The selections reprinted below are from *The Philosophy of Epicurus* translated by George K. Strodach.

Lucretius (c. 99–55) synthesized the philosophies of Epicurus and Democritus, and transmitted this knowledge from the Greek-speaking world into the Latin-speaking world. His "poem" *De Rerum Natura* ("On the Nature of Things") is a stylistic masterpiece of materialistic philosophy. The soul, says Lucretius, is made up of minute bodies which are dispersed at the time of death. This, of course, confirms Epicurus' view that death, being the absence of perception, should not concern us. The following selection is from *On the Nature of Things* reprinted from *The Stoic and Epicurean Philosophers,* edited by Whitney J. Oates.

3. The Christian philosophers of this era sought to reconcile Greek thought about death and the immortality of the soul with such Christian doctrines as the Trinity, heaven and hell, man's redemption, grace, the last judgment, and the resurrection.

St. Augustine (354–430) synthesized Christian teaching and Platonic philosophy. In his *City of God* he first defined human death, then philosophically justified his views. Human beings once had the potential for immortality, but lost it when they fell from God's grace through original sin. Mortality, then, is a punishment for this transgression. Augustine speaks of two types of death; the first occurs when the soul abandons the body, the second occurs when God abandons the soul. When seeking the philosophical justification for this view of death, Augustine turns to Plato's *Timaeus* (see Chapter 1) which says that God created the "lesser gods" with a union of body and soul which has the potential for being mortal (as is the case with human beings), yet they remain immortal because of God's will and purpose. The selections reprinted below are from Augustine's *City of God*, translated by Philip Levine.

4. The roots of skepticism have already been revealed in Chapter 1, when Socrates says that he does not know what death is, and in Chapter 2, when Confucius says "Not yet knowing life, how can I know death?" There are, perhaps, as many forms of skepticism as there are skeptics. Sextus Empiricus represents the Academic skeptics (Arcesilaus, Carneades, etc.) whose writings are no longer extant. Montaigne, on the other hand, is a representative of the "new skepticism" which reintroduced Classical Greek skepticism into sixteenth century Europe.

Sextus Empiricus (c. 160–210 A.D.) was a prolific writer whose extant works are the only currently available systematic account of Greek skepticism. This brief passage from his *Outlines of Pyrrhonism* (III. 226–232), observes various customs regarding the dead (including cannibalism), and concludes that since deaths are largely matters of convention, we should not think death a naturally dreadful thing. What follows is from *Sextus Empiricus*, with an English translation by R. G. Bury.

Michel de Montaigne, the French essayist, was born in 1533. His wit, charm, and philosophical disposition to Classical skepticism, are evident throughout his many essays. The style of these essays makes them easy and enjoyable to read. He was an observer of Nature, and this is a central theme that connects the wide variety of topics which he embraced. Montaigne adopted the Greek skeptics' method of rigorously doubting philosophical claims, religious dogma, scientific truths, and especially all superstition and supernaturalism. His most important philosophical contribution, the "Apology for Raimond Sebond," would later affect Descartes.

His most popular essay, however, undoubtedly is "That to Philosophize is to Learn to Die." This essay abounds in anecdotes, insightful observations, and relevant quotations from Horace, Virgil, and Lucretius. "That to Philosophize is to Learn to Die" is Montaigne at his best, advocating a continual consciousness of death throughout life. In this manner death is to be understood as a natural function of life; awareness of death affirms life and eliminates the fear of dying. Death, like birth, is part of Nature's way. No one is immune; and whether one dies from being struck on the head from "a tortoise dropped by a flying eagle" like Aeschylus, or "between women's thighs," like Cornelius Gallus the prator; "What does it matter," Montaigne asks, "how it happens, provided we do not worry about it."

"That to Philosophize is to Learn to Die," reprinted below in its entirety, was translated by Donald M. Frame, from *The Complete Essays of Montaigne.*

References

Bury, R. G., tr. *Sextus Empiricus,* Vol. 1., London: William Heinemann, 1933, pp. 477–81.

Frame, Donald M., tr., *The Complete Essays of Montaigne.* Stanford, CA: Stanford University Press, 1958, pp. 56–68.

Long, George, tr. *The Meditations of Marcus Aurelius.* NY: P. F. Collier & Son, 1909.

Oates, Whitney, ed. *The Stoic and Epicurean Philosophers.* NY: Random House, 1940, Book III (397–1094).

Oldfather, W. A. tr., *Epictetus,* 2 vols. Cambridge: Harvard University Press, 1946.

Saint Augustine, *City of God,* Vol. IV, Bk. 13., tr. Philip Levine. Cambridge: Harvard University Press, 1966.

Strodach, George K. tr., *The Philosophy of Epicurus.* Evanston, IL: Northwestern University Press, 1963.

EPICTETUS

from *Arrian's Discourses*

This is what it means to have rehearsed the lessons one ought to rehearse, to have set desire and aversion free from every hindrance and made them proof against chance. I must die. If forthwith, I die; and if a little later, I will take lunch now, since the hour for lunch has come, and afterwards I will die at the appointed time. How? As becomes the man who is giving back that which was another's. (Bk. I, ch. 1, 31–32)

And, in brief, it is neither death, nor exile, nor toil, nor any such thing that is the cause of our doing, or of our not doing, anything, but only our opinions and the decisions of our will. (Bk. I, ch. 11, 33)

When death appears to be an evil, we must have ready at hand the argument that it is our duty to avoid evils, and that death is an inevitable thing. For what can I do? . . . And where can I go to escape death? Show me the country, show me the people to whom I may go, upon whom death does not come; show me a magic charm against it. If I have none, what do you wish me to do? I cannot avoid death. Instead of avoiding the fear of it, shall I die in lamentation and trembling? For the origin of sorrow is this—to wish for something that does not come to pass. (Bk. I, ch. 27, 7–10)

For it is not death or hardship that is a fearful thing, but the fear of hardship or death. That is why we praise the man who said "Not death is dreadful, but a shameful death." Our confidence ought, therefore, to be turned toward death, and our caution toward the fear of death; whereas we do just the opposite—in the face of death we turn to flight, but to the formation of a judgment about death we manifest carelessness, disregard, and unconcern. But Socrates did well to call such things "bugbears." For just as masks appear fearful and terrible to children because of inexperience, in some such manner we also are affected by bugbears . . . What is death? A bugbear. Turn it about and learn what it is; see, it does not bite. The paltry body must be separated from the bit of spirit, either now or later, just as it existed apart from it before. Why are you grieved, then, if it be separated now? For if it be not separated now, it will be later. (Bk. II, ch. 1, 13–18)

We act very much as though we were on a voyage. What is possible for me? To select the helmsman, the sailors, the day, the moment. Then a storm comes down upon us. Very well, what further concern have I? For my part has been fulfilled. The business belongs to someone else, that is, the helmsman. But, more than that, the ship goes down. What, then, have I to do? What I can; that is the only thing I do; I drown without fear, neither shrieking nor crying out against God, but recognizing that what is born must also perish. For I am not eternal, but a man; a part of the whole, as an hour is part of a day. I must come on as the hour and like an hour pass away. What difference, then, is it to me how I pass away, whether by drowning or by a fever? For by something of the sort I must needs pass away. (Bk. II, ch. 5, 10–14)

What did you see? A man in grief over the death of his child? Apply your rule. Death lies outside the province of the moral purpose. Out of the way with it. (Bk. III, ch. 3, 15)

Do you not know that disease and death needs must overtake us, no matter what we are doing? They overtake the farmer at his work in the fields, the sailor on the sea. What do you wish to be doing when it overtakes you? For no matter what you do you will have to be overtaken by death. If you have anything better to be doing when you are so overtaken, get to work on that.

As for me, I would fain that death overtook me occupied with nothing but my own moral purpose, trying to make it tranquil, unhampered, unconstrained, free. This is what I wish to be engaged in when death finds me, so that I may be able to say to God, "Have I in any respect transgressed Thy commands? Have I in any respect misused the resources which Thou gavest me, or used my senses to no purpose . . . And now it is Thy will that I leave this festival; I go, I am full of gratitude to Thee that Thou hast deemed me worthy to take part in this festival with Thee, and to see Thy works, and to understand Thy governance." Be this my thought, this my writing, this my reading, when death comes upon me. (Bk. III, ch. 5, 6–11)

. . . If you have fever in the right way, you perform the things expected of the man who has a fever. What does it mean to have fever in the right way? Not to blame God, or man, not to be overwhelmed by what happens to you, to await death bravely and in the right way, to do what is enjoined upon you; when your physician comes to see you, not to be afraid of what he will say, and at the same time not to be carried away with joy, if he says, "You are doing splendidly"; for what good to you lay in that remark? Why, when you were well, what good was it to you? It means not to be downhearted, too, if he says, "You are in a bad way." For what does it mean to be in a bad way? That you are close to a separation of the soul from the body. What, then, is terrifying about that? If you do not draw near now, will you not draw near later? And is the universe going to be upset when you die? (Bk. III, ch. 10, 12–15)

"Touch what you will," the saying goes, "and it will turn into gold." Nay, but bring whatever you will and I will turn it into a good. Bring disease, bring death, bring poverty reviling, peril of life in court; all these things will become helpful at a touch from the magic wand of Hermes. "What will you make of death?" Why, what else but make it your glory, or an opportunity for you to show in deed thereby what sort of person a man is who follows the will of nature. "What will you make of disease?" I will show its character, I will shine in it, I will be firm, I will be serene, I will not fawn upon my physician, I will not pray for death. (Bk. III, ch. 20, 12–15)

In the first place, then, you must make your governing principle pure, and you must make the following your plan of life: "From now on my mind is the material with which I have to work, as the carpenter has his timbers, the shoemaker his hides; my business is to make the right use of my impressions. My paltry body is nothing to me; the parts of it are nothing to me. Death? Let it come when it will, whether it be the death of the whole or some part. (Bk. III, ch. 22, 19–22)

. . . And what is also the end of illness?—Anything but death? Will you, then, realize that this epitome of all the ills that befall man, of his ignoble spirit, and his cowardice, is not death, but it is rather the fear of death? Against this fear, then, I would have you discipline yourself, toward this let all your reasoning tend, your exercises, your reading; and then you will know that this is the only way in which men will achieve freedom. (Bk. III, ch. 26, 38–39)

Why, since you have to die in any event, you must be found doing something or other—farming, or digging, or engaged in commerce, or holding a consulship, or suffering with dyspepsia or dysentery. What is it, then, you wish to be doing when death finds you? I for my part should wish it to be some work that befits a man, something beneficent, that promotes the common welfare, or is noble. But if I cannot be found doing such great things as these, I should like at least to be engaged upon that which is free from hindrance, that which is given me to do, and that is, correcting myself, as I strive to perfect the faculty which deals with the external impressions, labouring to achieve calm, while yet giving to each of my human relationships its due. (Bk. IV, ch. 10, 11–13)

If a man dies young, he blames the gods (because he is carried off before his time. But if a man fails to die when he is old, he too blames the gods), because, when it was long since time for him to rest, he has trouble; yet none the less, when death draws nigh, he wishes to live, and sends for the doctor, and implores him to spare no zeal and pains. People are very strange, he used to say, wishing neither to live nor to die. (From *Fragments*, number 24)

The Enchiridion

III

With regard to whatever objects either delight the mind or contribute to use or are tenderly beloved, remind yourself of what nature they are, beginning with the merest trifles: if you have a favorite cup, that it is but a cup of which you are fond of—for thus if it is broken, you can bear it; if you embrace your child or your wife, that you embrace a mortal—and thus, if either of them dies, you can bear it.

V

Men are disturbed not by things, but by the views which they take of things. Thus death is nothing terrible, else it would have appeared so to Socrates. But the terror consists in our notion of death, that it is terrible. When, therefore, we are hindered or disturbed, or grieved, let us never impute it to others, but to ourselves—that is, to our own views. It is the action of an uninstructed person to reproach others for his own misfortunes; of one entering upon instruction, to reproach himself; and one perfectly instructed, to reproach neither others nor himself.

XI

Never say of anything, "I have lost it," but, "I have restored it." Has your child died? It is restored. Has you wife died? She is restored. Has your estate been taken away? That likewise is restored. "But it was a bad man who took it." What is it to you by whose hands he who gave it has demanded it again? While he permits you to possess it, hold it as something not your own, as do travelers at an inn.

XIV

If you wish your children and your wife and your friends to live forever, you are foolish, for you wish things to be in your power which are not so, and what belongs to others to be your own. So likewise, if you wish your servant to be without fault, you are foolish, for you wish vice not to be vice but something else. But if you wish not to be disappointed in your desires, that is in your power. A man's master is he who is able to confer or remove whatever that man seeks or shuns. Whoever then would be free, let him wish nothing, let him decline nothing, which depends on others; else he must necessarily be a slave.

XXI

Let death and exile, and all other things which appear terrible, be daily before your eyes, but death chiefly; and you will never entertain an abject thought, not too eagerly covet anything.

XXVI

The will of nature may be learned from things upon which we are all agreed. As when our neighbor's boy has broken a cup, or the like, we are ready at once to say, "These are casualties that will happen;" be assured, then, that when your own cup is likewise broken, you ought to be affected just as when another's cup was broken. Now apply this to greater things. Is the child or the wife of another dead? There is no one who would not say, "This is an accident of mortality." But if anyone's own child happens to die, it is immediately, "Alas! how wretched am I!" It should be always remembered how we are affected on hearing the same thing concerning others.

MARCUS AURELIUS ANTONINUS

from
The Meditations

Since it is possible that thou mayest depart from life this very moment, regulate every act and thought accordingly. But to go away from among men, if there are gods, is not a thing to be afraid of, for the gods will not involve thee in evil; but if indeed they do not exist, or if they have no concern about human affairs, what is it to me to live in a universe devoid of gods or devoid of providence? But in truth they do exist, and they do care for human things, and they have put all the means in man's power to enable him not to fall into real evils. And as to the rest, if there was anything evil, they would have provided for this also, that it should be altogether in a man's power not to fall into it. Now, that which does not make a man worse, how can it make a man's life worse? But neither through ignorance, nor having the knowledge, but not the power to guard against or correct these things, is it possible that the nature of the universe has overlooked them; nor is it possible that it has made so great a mistake, either through want of power or want of skill, that good and evil should happen indiscriminately to the good and the bad. But death certainly, and life, honour and dishonour, pain and pleasure, all these things equally happen to good men and bad, being things which make us neither better or worse. Therefore they are neither good nor evil.

How quickly all these things disappear, in the universe the bodies themselves, but in time the remembrance of them; what is the nature of all sensible things, and particularly those which attract with the bait of pleasure or terrify by pain, or are noised about by vapoury fame; how worthless, and contemptible, and sordid, and perishable, and dead they are—all this is part of the intellectual faculty to observe. To observe, too, who these are whose opinions and voices give reputation; what death is, and the fact that, if a man looks at it in itself, and by the abstractive power of reflection resolves into their parts all things which present themselves to the imagination in it, he will then consider it to be nothing else than an operation of nature; and if anyone is afraid of an operation of nature he is a child. (Bk. II, ch. 11–12)

Of human life the time is a point, and the substance is in a flux, and the perception dull, and the composition of the whole body subject to putrefaction, and the soul a whirl, and fortune hard to divine, and fame a thing devoid of judgment. And, to say all in a word, everything which belongs to the body is a stream, and what belongs to the soul is a dream and a vapour, and life is a warfare and a stranger's sojourn . . . (Bk. II, ch. 17)

Hippocrates after curing many diseases himself fell sick and died . . . Heraclitus, after so many speculations on the conflagration of the universe, was filled with water internally and died smeared all over with mud. And lice destroyed Democritus; and other lice killed Socrates. What means all this? Thou hast embarked, thou hast made the voyage, thou art come to shore; get out. If indeed to another life, there is no want of gods, not even there. But if to a state without sensation, thou wilt cease to be held by pains and pleasures, and to be a slave to the vessel which is as much inferior as that which serves it is superior; for the one is intelligence and deity; the other is earth and corruption. (Bk. III, ch. 3)

Death is such as generation is, a mystery of nature; a composition out of the same elements, and a decomposition into the same; and altogether not a thing of which any man should be ashamed, for it is not contrary to [the nature of] a reasonable animal, and not contrary to the reason of our constitution. (Bk. IV, ch. 5)

Do not act as if thou wert going to live ten thousand years. Death hangs over thee. While thou livest, while it is in thy power, be good. (Bk. IV, ch. 17)

Think continually how many physicians are dead after often contracting their eyebrows over the sick; and how many astrologers after predicting with great pretensions the death of others; and how many philosophers after endless discourses on death or immortality . . . Add to the reckoning all whom thou hast known, one after another. One man after burying another has been laid out dead, and another buries him; and all this in a short time. To conclude, always observe how ephemeral and worthless human things are, and what was yesterday a little mucus, tomorrow will be a mummy or ashes. Pass then through this little space of time conformably to nature, and end thy journey in content, just as an olive falls off when it is ripe, blessing nature who produced it, and thanking the tree on which it grew. (Bk. IV, ch. 48)

Death is the cessation of the impressions through the senses, and of the pulling of the strings which move the appetites, and of the discursive movements of the thoughts, and of the service to the flesh. (Bk. VI, ch. 28)

About death: whether it is a dispersion, or a resolution into atoms, or annihilation, it is either extinction or change. (Bk. VII, ch. 32)

He who fears death either fears the loss of sensation or a different kind of sensation. But if thou shalt have no sensation, neither wilt thou feel any harm; and if thou shalt acquire another kind of sensation, thou wilt be a different kind of living being, and thou wilt not cease to live. (Bk. VII, ch. 58)

Do not despise death, but be well content with it, since this too is one of those things which nature wills. For such as it is to be young and to grow old, and to increase and to reach maturity, and to have teeth and beard and gray hairs, and to beget, and to be pregnant, and to bring forth, and all other natural operations which the seasons of thy life bring, such also is dissolution. This, then, is consistent with the character of a reflecting man, to be neither careless nor impatient nor contemptuous with respect to death, but to wait for it as one of the operations of nature. As thou now waitest for the time when the child shall come out of thy wife's womb, so be ready for the time when thy soul shall fall out of this envelope . . . (Bk. IX, ch. 3)

EPICURUS

Letter to Menoeceus

No one should postpone the study of philosophy when he is young, nor should he weary of it when he becomes mature, because the search for mental health is never untimely or out of season. To say that the time to study philosophy has not yet arrived or that it is passed is like saying that the time for happiness is not yet at hand or is no longer present. Thus both the young and the mature should pursue philosophy, the latter in order to be rejuvenated as they age by the blessings that accrue from pleasurable past experience, and the youthful in order to become mature immediately through having no fear of the future. Hence we should make a practice of the things that make for happiness, for assuredly when we have this we have everything, and we do everything we can to get it when we don't have it.

. . . You should accustom yourself to believing that death means nothing to us, since every good and every evil lies in sensation; but death is the privation of sensation. Hence a correct comprehension of the fact that death means nothing to us makes the mortal aspect of life pleasurable, not by conferring on us a boundless period of time but by removing the yearning for deathlessness. There is nothing fearful in living for the person who has really laid hold of the fact that there is nothing fearful in not living. So it is silly for a person to say that he dreads death—not because it will be painful when it arrives but because it pains him now as a future certainty; for that which makes no trouble for us when it arrives is a meaningless pain when we await it. This, the most horrifying of evils, means nothing to us, then, because so long as we are existent death is not present and whenever it is present we are nonexistent. Thus it is of no concern either to the living or to those who have completed their lives. For the former it is nonexistent, and the latter are themselves nonexistent.

Most people, however, recoil from death as though it were the greatest of evils; at other times they welcome it as the end-all of life's ills. The sophisticated person, on the other hand, neither begs off from living nor dreads not living. Life is not a stumbling block to him, nor does he regard not being alive as any sort of evil. As in the case of food he prefers the most savory dish to merely the larger portion, so in the case of time he garners to himself the most agreeable moments rather than the longest span.

Anyone who urges the youth to lead a good life but counsels the older man to end his life in good style is silly, not merely because of the welcome character of life but because of the fact that living well and dying well are one and the same discipline. Much worse off, however, is the person who says it were well not to have been born "but once born to pass through Hades' portals as swiftly as may be." Now if he says such a thing from inner persuasion why does he not withdraw from life? Everything is in readiness for him once he has firmly resolved on this course. But if he speaks facetiously he is a trifler standing in the midst of men who do not welcome him.

It should be borne in mind, then, that the time to come is neither ours nor altogether not ours. In this way we shall neither expect the future outright as something destined to be nor despair of it as something absolutely not destined to be.

Leading Doctrines

2. Death means nothing to us, because that which has been broken down into atoms has no sensation and that which has no sensation is no concern of ours.

11. We would have no need for natural science unless we were worried by apprehensiveness regarding the heavenly bodies, by anxiety about the meaning of death, and also by our failure to understand the limitations of pain and desire.

20. The body takes the limits of pleasure to be infinite, and infinite time would provide such pleasure. But the mind has provided us with the complete life by a rational examination of the body's goal and limitations and by dispelling our fears about a life after death; and so we no longer need unlimited time. On the other hand, it does not avoid pleasure, nor, when conditions occasion our departure from life, does it

come to the end in a manner that would suggest that it had fallen short in any way of the best possible existence.

Vatican Collection of Aphorisms

14. We are born once. We cannot be born a second time, and throughout eternity we shall of necessity no longer exist. You have no power over the morrow, and yet you put off your pleasure. Life is ruined by procrastination, and every one of us dies deep in his affairs.

31. It is possible to get protection against other things, but when it comes to death, all of us human beings live in a city without walls.

LUCRETIUS

from On the Nature of Things

The mind has more to do with holding the fastnesses of life and has more sovereign sway over it than the power of the soul. For without the understanding and the mind no part of the soul can maintain itself in the frame the smallest fraction of time, but follows at once in the other's train and passes away into the air and leaves the cold limbs in the chill of death. But he abides in life whose mind and understanding continue to stay with him: though the trunk is mangled with its limbs shorn all round about it, after the soul has been taken away on all sides and been severed from the limbs, the trunk yet lives and inhales the ethereal airs of life. When robbed, if not of the whole, yet of a large portion of the soul, it still lingers in and cleaves to life; just as, after the eye has been lacerated all round if the pupil has continued uninjured, the living power of sight remains, provided always you do not destroy the whole ball of the eye and pare close round the pupil and leave only it; for that will not be done even to the ball without the entire destruction of the eye. But if that middle portion of the eye, small as it is, is eaten into, the sight is gone at once and darkness ensues, though a man have the bright ball quite unimpaired. On such terms of union soul and mind are ever bound to each other.

Now mark me: that you may know that the minds and light souls of living creatures have birth and are mortal, I will go on to set forth verses worthy of your attention, got together by long study and invented with welcome effort. Do you mind to link to one name both of them alike, and when for instance I shall choose to speak of the soul, showing it to be mortal, believe that I speak of the mind as well, inasmuch as both make up one thing and are one united substance. First of all then since I have shown the soul to be fine and to be formed of minute bodies and made up of much smaller first-beginnings than is the liquid of water or mist or smoke:—for it far surpasses these in nimbleness and is moved, when struck by a far slenderer cause; inasmuch as it is moved by images of smoke and mist; as when for instance sunk in sleep we see altars steam forth their heat and send up their smoke on high; for beyond a doubt images are begotten for us from these things:—well then since you see on the vessels being shattered the water flow away on all sides, and since mist and smoke pass away into air, believe that the soul too is shed abroad and perishes much more quickly and dissolves sooner into its first bodies, when once it has been taken out of the limbs of a man and has withdrawn. For, when the body that serves for its vessel cannot hold it, if shattered from any cause and rarefied by the withdrawal of blood from the veins, how can you believe that this soul can be held by any air? How can that air which is rarer than our body hold it in?

Again we perceive that the mind is begotten along with the body and grows up together with it and becomes old along with it. For even as children go about with a tottering and weakly body, so slender sagacity of mind follows along with it; then when their life has reached the maturity of confirmed strength, the judgement too is greater and the power of the mind more developed. Afterwards when the body has been shattered by the mastering might of time and the frame has drooped with its forces dulled, then the intellect halts, the tongue dotes, the mind gives way, all faculties fail, and are found wanting at the same time. It naturally follows then that the whole nature of the soul is dissolved, like smoke, into the high air; since we see it is begotten along with the body and grows up along with it and, as I have shown, breaks down at the same time worn out with age.

Moreover we see that even as the body is liable to violent diseases and severe pain, so is the mind to sharp cares and grief and fear; it naturally follows therefore that it is its partner in death as well. Again in diseases of the body the mind often wanders and goes astray; for it loses its reason and drivels in its speech and often in a profound lethargy is carried into deep and never-ending sleep with drooping eyes and head; out of which it neither hears the voices nor can recognise the faces of those who stand round calling it back to life and bedewing with tears, face and cheeks. Therefore you must admit that the mind too dissolves, since the infection of disease reaches to it; for pain and disease are both forgers of death: a truth we have fully learned ere now by the death of many. Again, when the pungent strength of wine has entered into a man and its spirit has been infused into and transmitted through his veins, why is it that a heaviness of the limbs follows along with this, his legs are hampered as he reels about, his tongue falters, his mind is besotted, his eyes swim, shouting, hiccuping, wranglings are rife, together with all the other usual concomitants, why is all this, if not because the overpowering violence of the wine is wont to disorder the soul within the body? But whenever things can be disordered and hampered, they give token that if a somewhat more potent cause gained an entrance, they would perish and be robbed of all further existence. Moreover it often happens that some one constrained by the violence of disease suddenly drops down before our eyes, as by a stroke of lightning, and foams at the mouth, moans and shivers through his frame, loses his reason, stiffens his muscles, is racked, gasps for breath fitfully, and wearies his limbs with tossing. Sure enough, because the violence of the disease spreads itself through his frame and disorders him, he foams as he tries to eject his soul, just as in the salt sea the waters boil with the mastering might of the winds. A moan too is forced out, because the limbs are seized with pain, and mainly because seeds of voice are driven forth and are carried in a close mass out by the mouth, the road which they are accustomed to take and where they have a well-paved way. Loss of reason follows, because the powers of the mind and soul are disordered and, as I have shown, are riven and forced asunder, torn to pieces by the same baneful malady. Then after the cause of the disease has bent its course back and the acrid humours of the distempered body return to their hiding-places, then he first gets up like one reeling, and by little and little comes back into full possession of his senses and regains his soul. Since therefore even within the body mind and soul are harassed by such violent distempers and so miserably racked by sufferings, why believe that they without the body in the open air can continue existence battling with fierce winds? And since we perceive that the mind is healed like the sick body, and we see that it can be altered by medicine, this too gives warning that the mind has a mortal existence. For it is natural that whosoever essays and attempts to change the mind or seeks to alter any other nature you like, should add new parts or change the arrangement of the present, or withdraw in short some tittle from the sum. But that which is immortal wills not to have its parts transposed nor any addition to be made nor one tittle to ebb away; for whenever a thing changes and quits its proper limits, this change is at once the death of that which was before. Therefore the mind, whether it is sick or whether it is altered by medicine, alike, as I have shown, gives forth mortal symptoms. So invariably is truth found to make head against false reason and to cut off all retreat from the assailant and by a two-fold refutation to put falsehood to rout.

Again we often see a man pass gradually away and limb by limb lose vital sense; first the toes of his feet and the nails turn livid, then the feet and shanks die, then next the steps of chilly death creep with slow pace over the other members. Therefore since the nature of the soul is rent and passes away and does not at one time stand forth in its entireness, it must be reckoned mortal. But if haply you suppose that it can draw itself in through the whole frame and mass its parts together and in this way withdraw sense from all the limbs, yet then that spot into which so great a store of soul is gathered, ought to show itself in possession of a greater amount of sense. But as this is nowhere found, sure enough as we said before, it is torn in pieces and scattered abroad, and therefore dies. Moreover if I were pleased for the moment to grant what is false and admit that the soul might be collected in one mass in the body of those who leave the light dying piecemeal, even then you must admit the soul to be mortal; and it makes no difference whether it perish dispersed in air, or gathered into one lump out of all its parts lose all feeling, since sense ever more and more fails the whole man throughout and less and less of life remains throughout.

And since the mind is one part of a man which remains fixed in a particular spot, just as are the ears and eyes and the other senses which guide and direct life; and just as the hand or eye or nose when separated from us cannot feel and exist apart, but in however short a time wastes away in putrefaction, thus the mind cannot exist by itself without the body and the man's self which as you see serves for the mind's vessel or any thing else you choose to imagine which implies a yet closer union with it, since the body is attached to it by the nearest ties.

Again the quickened powers of body and mind by their joint partnership enjoy health and life; for the nature of the mind cannot by itself alone without the body give forth vital motions nor can the body again bereft of the soul continue to exist and make use of its senses: just, you are to know, as the eye itself torn away from its roots cannot see anything when apart from the whole body, thus the soul and mind cannot it is plain do anything by themselves. Sure enough, because mixed up through veins and flesh, sinews and bones, their first-beginnings are confined by all the body and are not free to bound away leaving great spaces between, therefore thus shut in they make those sense-giving motions which they cannot make after death when forced out of the body into the air by reason that they are not then confined in a like manner; for the air will be a body and a living thing, if the soul shall be able to keep itself together and to enclose in it those motions which it used before to perform in the sinews and within the body. Moreover even while it yet moves within the confines of life, often the soul shaken from some cause or other is seen to wish to pass out and be loosed from the whole body, the features are seen to droop as at the last hour and all

the limbs to sink flaccid over the bloodless trunk: just as happens, when
the phrase is used, the mind is in a bad way, or the soul is quite gone;
when all is hurry and every one is anxious to keep from parting the last
tie of life; for then the mind and the power of the soul are shaken
throughout and both are quite loosened together with the body; so that
a cause somewhat more powerful can quite break them up. Why doubt
I would ask that the soul when driven forth out of the body, when in the
open air, feeble as it is, stript of its covering, not only cannot continue
through eternity, but is unable to hold together the smallest fraction of
time? Therefore, again and again I say, when the enveloping body has
been all broken up and the vital airs have been forced out, you must
admit that the senses of the mind and the soul are dissolved, since the
cause of destruction is one and inseparable for both body and soul.

Again since the body is unable to bear the separation of the soul
without rotting away in a noisome stench, why doubt that the power of
the soul gathering itself up from the inmost depths of body has oozed
out and dispersed like smoke, and that the crumbling body has changed
and tumbled in with so total a ruin for this reason because its foundations throughout are stirred from their places, the soul oozing out
abroad through the frame, through all the winding passages which are
in the body, and all openings? So that in ways manifold you may learn
that the nature of the soul has been divided piecemeal and gone forth
throughout the frame, and that it has been torn to shreds within the
body, ere it glided forth and swam out into the air. For no one when
dying appears to feel the soul go forth entire from his whole body or
first mount up to the throat and gullet, but all feel it fail in that part
which lies in a particular quarter; just as they know that the senses as well
suffer dissolution each in its own place. But if our mind were immortal,
it would not when dying complain so much of its dissolution, as of
passing abroad and quitting its vesture, like a snake.

Again why are the mind's understanding and judgement never
begotten in the head or feet or hands, but cling in all alike to one spot
and fixed quarter, if it be not that particular places are assigned for the
birth of everything, and nature has determined where each is to
continue to exist after it is born? Our body then must follow the same
law and have such a manifold organisation of parts, that no perverted
arrangement of its members shall ever show itself: so invariably effect
follows cause, nor is flame wont to be born in rivers nor cold in fire.

Again if the nature of the soul is immortal and can feel when
separated from our body, methinks we must suppose it to be provided
with five senses; and in no other way can we picture to ourselves souls
below flitting about Acheron. Painters therefore and former genera-

tions of writers have thus represented souls provided with senses. But neither eyes nor nose nor hand can exist for the soul apart from the body nor can tongue, nor can ears perceive by the sense of hearing or exist for the soul by themselves apart from the body.

And since we perceive that vital sense is in the whole body and we see that it is all endowed with life, if on a sudden any force with swift blow shall have cut it in twain so as quite to dissever the two halves, the power of the soul will without doubt at the same time be cleft and cut asunder and dashed in twain together with the body. But that which is cut and divides into any parts, you are to know disclaims for itself an everlasting nature. Stories are told how scythed chariots reeking with indiscriminate slaughter often lop off limbs so instantaneously that that which has fallen down lopped off from the frame is seen to quiver on the ground, while yet the mind and faculty of the man from the suddenness of the mischief cannot feel the pain; and because his mind once for all is wholly given to the business of fighting, with what remains of his body he mingles in the fray and carnage, and often perceives not that the wheels and devouring scythes have carried off among the horses' feet his left arm shield and all; another sees not that his right arm has dropped from him, while he mounts and presses forward. Another tries to get up after he has lost his leg, while the dying foot quivers with its toes on the ground close by. The head too when cut off from the warm and living trunk retains on the ground the expression of life and open eyes, until it has yielded up all the remnants of soul. To take another case, if, as a serpent's tongue is quivering, as its tail is darting out from its long body, you choose to chop with an axe into many pieces both tail and body, you will see all the separate portions thus cut off writhing under the fresh wound and bespattering the earth with gore, the fore part with the mouth making for its own hinder part, to allay with burning bite the pain of the wound with which it has been smitten. Shall we say then that there are entire souls in all those pieces? why from that argument it will follow that one living creature had many souls in its body; and this being absurd, therefore the soul which was one has been divided together with the body; therefore each alike must be reckoned mortal, since each is alike chopped up into many pieces.

Again if the nature of the soul is immortal and makes its way into our body at the time of birth, why are we unable to remember besides the time already gone, and why do we retain no traces of past actions? If the power of the mind has been so completely changed, that all remembrance of past things is lost, that methinks differs not widely from death; therefore you must admit that the soul which was before has perished and that which now is has now been formed.

Again if the quickened power of the mind is wont to be put into us after our body is fully formed, at the instant of our birth and our crossing the threshold of life, it ought agreeably to this to live not in such a way as to seem to have grown with the body and together with its members within the blood, but as in a den apart by and to itself: the very contrary to what undoubted fact teaches; for it is so closely united with the body throughout the veins, flesh, sinews, and bones, that the very teeth have a share of sense; as their aching proves and the sharp twinge of cold water and the crunching of a rough stone, when it has got into them out of bread. Wherefore, again and again I say, we must believe souls to be neither without a birth nor exempted from the law of death; for we must not believe that they could have been so completely united with our bodies, if they found their way into them from without, nor, since they are so closely inwoven with them, does it appear that they can get out unharmed and unloose themselves unscathed from all the sinews and bones and joints. But if haply you believe that the soul finds its way in from without and is wont to ooze through all our limbs, so much the more it will perish thus blended with the body; for what oozes through another is dissolved, and therefore dies. As food distributed through all the cavities of the body, while it is transmitted into the limbs and the whole frame, is destroyed and furnishes out of itself the matter of another nature, thus the soul and mind, though they pass entire into a fresh body, yet in oozing through it are dissolved, whilst there are transmitted so to say into the frame through all the cavities those particles of which this nature of mind is formed, which now is sovereign in our body, being born out of that soul which then perished when dispersed through the frame. Wherefore the nature of the soul is seen to be neither without a birthday nor exempt from death.

Again are seeds of the soul left in the dead body or not? If they are left and remain in it, the soul cannot fairly be deemed immortal, since it has withdrawn lessened by the loss of some parts; but if when taken away from the yet untainted limbs it has fled so entirely away as to leave in the body no parts of itself, whence do carcases exude worms from the now rank flesh and whence does such a swarm of living things, boneless and bloodless, surge through the heaving frame? But if haply you believe that souls find their way into worms from without and can severally pass each into a body and you make no account of why many thousands of souls meet together in a place from which one has withdrawn, this question at least must, it seems, be raised and brought to a decisive test, whether souls hunt out the several seeds of worms and build for themselves a place to dwell in, or find their way into bodies fully formed so to say. But why they should on their part make a body or take such trouble, cannot be explained; since being without a body they are not plagued as they flit about with diseases and cold and hunger, the body being more akin to, more troubled by such infirmities, and by its contact with it the mind suffering many ills. Nevertheless be it ever so expedient for them to make a body, when they are going to enter, yet clearly there is no way by which they can do so. Therefore souls do not make for themselves bodies and limbs; no nor can they by any method find their way into bodies after they are fully formed; for they will neither be able to unite themselves with a nice precision nor will any connexion of mutual sensation be formed between them.

Again why does untamed fierceness go along with the sullen brood of lions, cunning with foxes and proneness to flight with stags? And to take any other instance of the kind, why are all qualities engendered in the limbs and temper from the very commencement of life, if not because a fixed power of mind derived from its proper seed and breed grows up together with the whole body? If it were immortal and wont to pass into different bodies, living creatures would be of interchangeable dispositions; a dog of Hyrcanian breed would often fly before the attack of an antlered stag, a hawk would cower in mid air as it fled at the approach of a dove, men would be without reason, the savage races of wild beasts would have reason. For the assertion that an immortal soul is altered by a change of body is advanced on a false principle. What is changed is dissolved, and therefore dies: the parts are transposed and quit their former order; therefore they must admit of being dissolved too throughout the frame, in order at last to die one and all together with the body. But if they shall say that souls of men always go into human bodies, I yet will ask how it is a soul can change from wise to foolish, and no child has discretion, and why the mare's foal is not so well trained as the powerful strength of the horse. You may be sure they will fly to the subterfuge that the mind grows weakly in a weakly body. But granting this is so, you must admit the soul to be mortal, since changed so completely throughout the frame it loses its former life and sense. Then too in what way will it be able to grow in strength uniformly with its allotted body and reach the coveted flower of age, unless it shall be its partner at its first beginning? Or what means it by passing out from the limbs when decayed with age? Does it fear to remain shut up in a crumbling body, fear that its tenement, worn out by protracted length of days, bury it in its ruins? Why an immortal being incurs no risks.

Again for souls to stand by at the unions of Venus and the birth-throes of beasts seems to be passing absurd, for them the immortals to wait for mortal limbs in number numberless and struggle with one another in forward rivalry, which shall first and by preference have entrance in;

unless haply bargains are struck among the souls on these terms, that whichever in its flight shall first come up, shall first have right of entry, and that they shall make no trial at all of each other's strength.

Again a tree cannot exist in the ether, nor clouds in the deep sea nor can fishes live in the fields nor blood exist in woods nor sap in stones. Where each thing can grow and abide is fixed and ordained. Thus the nature of the mind cannot come into being alone without the body nor exist far away from the sinews and blood. But if (for this would be much more likely to happen than that) the force itself of the mind might be in the head or shoulders or heels or might be born in any other part of the body, it would after all be wont to abide in one and the same man or vessel. But since in our body even it is fixed and seen to be ordained where the soul and the mind can severally be and grow, it must still more strenuously be denied that it can abide and be born out of the body altogether. Therefore when the body has died, we must admit that the soul has perished, wrenched away throughout the body. To link forsooth a mortal thing with an everlasting and suppose that they can have sense in common and can be reciprocally acted upon, is sheer folly; for what can be conceived more incongruous, more discordant and inconsistent with itself, than a thing which is mortal, linked with an immortal and everlasting thing, trying in such union to weather furious storms? But if haply the soul is to be accounted immortal for this reason rather, because it is kept sheltered from death-bringing things, either because things hostile to its existence do not approach at all, or because those which do approach, in some way or other retreat discomfited before we can feel the harm they do, manifest experience proves that this can not be true. For besides that it sickens in sympathy with the maladies of the body, it is often attacked by that which frets it on the score of the future and keeps it on the rack of suspense and wears it out with cares; and when ill deeds are in the past, remorse for sins yet gnaws: then there is madness peculiar to the mind and forgetfulness of all things; then too it often sinks into the black waters of lethargy.

Death therefore to us is nothing, concerns us not a jot, since the nature of the mind is proved to be mortal; and as in time gone by we felt no distress, when the Poeni from all sides came together to do battle, and all things shaken by war's troublous uproar shuddered and quaked beneath high heaven, and mortal men were in doubt which of the two peoples it should be to whose empire all must fall by sea and land alike, thus when we shall be no more, when there shall have been a separation of body and soul, out of both of which we are each formed into a single being, to us, you may be sure, who then shall be no more, nothing whatever can happen to excite sensation, not if earth shall be mingled with sea and sea with heaven. And even supposing the nature of the mind and power of the soul do feel, after they have been severed from our body, yet that is nothing to us who by the binding tie of marriage between body and soul are formed each into one single being. And if time should gather up our matter after our death and put it once more into the position in which it now is, and the light of life be given to us again, this result even would concern us not at all, when the chain of our self-consciousness has once been snapped asunder. So now we give ourselves no concern about any self which we have been before, nor do we feel any distress on the score of that self. For when you look back on the whole past course of immeasurable time and think how manifold are the shapes which the motions of matter take, you may easily credit this too, that these very same seeds of which we now are formed, have often before been placed in the same order in which they now are; and yet we cannot recover this in memory: a break in our existence has been interposed, and all the motions have wandered to and fro far astray from the sensations they produced. For he whom evil is to befall, must in his own person exist at the very time it comes, if the misery and suffering are haply to have any place at all; but since death precludes this, and forbids him to be, upon whom the ills can be brought, you may be sure that we have nothing to fear after death, and that he who exists not, cannot become miserable, and that it matters not a whit whether he has been born into life at any other time, when immortal death has taken away his mortal life.

Therefore when you see a man bemoaning his hard case, that after death he shall either rot with his body laid in the grave or be devoured by flames or the jaws of wild beasts, you may be sure that his ring betrays a flaw and that there lurks in his heart a secret goad, though he himself declare that he does not believe that any sense will remain to him after death. He does not methinks really grant the conclusion which he professes to grant nor the principle on which he so professes, nor does he take and force himself root and branch out of life, but all unconsciously imagines something of self to survive. For when any one in life suggests to himself that birds and beasts will rend his body after death, he makes moan for himself: he does not separate himself from that self, nor withdraw himself fully from the body so thrown out, and fancies himself that other self and stands by and impregnates it with his own sense. Hence he makes much moan that he has been born mortal, and sees not that after real death there will be no other self to remain in life and lament to self that his own self has met death, and there to stand and grieve that his own self there lying is mangled or burnt. For if it is an evil after death to be pulled about by the devouring jaws of wild beasts, I cannot see why it should not be a cruel pain to be laid on fires and burn in hot flames, or to be placed in honey and stifled, or to stiffen with cold, stretched on the smooth surface of an icy slab of stone, or to be pressed down and crushed by a load of earth above.

'Now no more shall thy house admit thee with glad welcome, nor a most virtuous wife and sweet children run to be the first to snatch kisses and touch thy heart with a silent joy. No more mayst thou be prosperous in thy doings, a safeguard to thine own. One disastrous day has taken from thee luckless man in luckless wise all the many prizes of life.' This do men say; but add not thereto 'and now no longer does any craving for these things beset thee withal.' For if they could rightly perceive this in thought and follow up the thought in words, they would release themselves from great distress and apprehension of mind. 'Thou, even as now thou art, sunk in the sleep of death, shalt continue so to be all time to come, freed from all distressful pains; but we with a sorrow that would not be sated wept for thee, when close by thou didst turn to an ashen hue on thy appalling funeral pile, and no length of days shall pluck from our hearts our ever-during grief.' This question therefore should be asked of this speaker, what there is in it so passing bitter, if it come in the end to sleep and rest, that any one should pine in never-ending sorrow.

This too men often, when they have reclined at table cup in hand and shade their brows with crowns, love to say from the heart, 'short is this enjoyment for poor weak men; presently it will have been and never after may it be called back'. As if after their death it is to be one of their chiefest afflictions that thirst and parching drought is to burn them up hapless wretches, or a craving for any thing else is to beset them. What folly! no one feels the want of himself and life at the time when mind and body are together sunk in sleep; for all we care this sleep might be everlasting, no craving whatever for ourselves then moves us. And yet by no means do those first-beginnings throughout our frame wander at that time far away from their sense-producing motions, at the moment when a man starts up from sleep and collects himself. Death therefore must be thought to concern us much less, if less there can be than what we see to be nothing; for a greater dispersion of the mass of matter follows after death, and no one wakes up, upon whom the chill cessation of life has once come.

Once more, if the nature of things could suddenly utter a voice and in person could rally any of us in such words as these, 'what hast thou, O mortal, so much as heart, that thou goest such lengths in sickly sorrows? Why bemoan and bewail death? For say thy life past and gone has been welcome to thee and thy blessings have not all, as if they were poured into a perforated vessel, run through and been lost without avail: why not then take thy departure like a guest filled with life, and with resignation, thou fool, enter upon untroubled rest? But if all that thou hast enjoyed, has been squandered and lost, and life is a grievance, why seek to make any addition, to be wasted perversely in its turn and lost utterly without avail? Why not rather make an end of life and travail? For there is nothing more which I can contrive and discover for thee to give pleasure: all things are ever the same. Though thy body is not yet decayed with years nor thy frame worn out and exhausted, yet all things remain the same, ay though in length of life thou shouldst outlast all races of things now living, nay even more if thou shouldst never die,' what answer have we to make save this, that nature sets up against us a well-founded claim and puts forth in her pleading a true indictment? If however one of greater age and more advanced in years should complain and lament poor wretch his death more than is right, would she not with greater cause raise her voice and rally him in sharp accents, 'Away from this time forth with thy tears, rascal; a truce to thy complainings: thou decayest after full enjoyment of all the prizes of life. But because thou ever yearnest for what is not present, and despisest what is, life has slipped from thy grasp unfinished and unsatisfying, and or ever thou thoughtest, death has taken his stand at thy pillow, before thou canst take thy departure sated and filled with good things. Now however, resign all things unsuited to thy age, and with a good grace up and greatly go: thou must.' With good reason methinks she would bring her charge, with reason rally and reproach; for old things give way and are supplanted by new without fail, and one thing must ever be replenished out of other things; and no one is delivered over to the pit and black Tartarus: matter is needed for after generations to grow; all of which though will follow thee when they have finished their term of life; and thus it is that all these no less than thou have before this come to an end and hereafter will come to an end. Thus one thing will never cease to rise out of another, and life is granted to none in fee-simple, to all in usufruct. Think too how the bygone antiquity of everlasting time before our birth was nothing to us. Nature therefore holds this up to us as a mirror of the time yet to come after our death. Is there aught in this that looks appalling, aught that wears an aspect of gloom? Is it not more untroubled than any sleep?

And those things sure enough, which are fabled to be in the deep of Acheron, do all exist for us in this life. No Tantalus, numbed by groundless terror, as the story is, fears poor wretch a huge stone hanging in air; but in life rather a baseless dread of the god vexes mortals: the fall they fear is such fall of luck as chance brings to each. Nor do birds eat a way into Tityos laid in Acheron, nor can they sooth to say find during eternity food to peck under his large breast. However huge the bulk of body he extends, though such as to take up with out-spread limbs not nine acres merely, but the whole earth, yet will he not be able to endure everlasting pain and supply food from his own body for ever. But he is for us a Tityos, whom, as he grovels in love, vultures rend and bitter bitter anguish eats up or troubled thoughts from any other passion do rive. In life too we have a Sisyphus before our eyes who is bent on asking from the people the rods and cruel axes, and always retires defeated and disappointed. For to ask for power, which empty as it is is never given, and always in the chase of it to undergo severe toil, this is forcing up-hill with much effort a stone which after all rolls back again from the summit and seeks in headlong haste the levels of the plain. Then to be ever feeding the thankless nature of the mind, and never to fill it full and sate it with good things, as the seasons of the year do for us, when they come round and bring their fruits and varied delights, though after all we are never filled with the enjoyments of life, this methinks is to do what is told of the maidens in the flower of their age, to keep pouring water into a perforated vessel which in spite of all can never be filled full. Moreover Cerberus and the furies and yon privation of light are idle tales, as well as all the rest, Ixion's wheel and black Tartarus belching forth hideous fires from his throat: things which nowhere are nor sooth to say can be. But there is in life a dread of punishment for evil deeds, signal as the deeds are signal, and for atonement of guilt, the prison and the frightful hurling down from the rock, scourgings, executioners, the dungeon of the doomed, the pitch, the metal plate, torches; and even though these are wanting, yet the conscience-stricken mind through boding fears applies to itself goads and frightens itself with whips, and sees not meanwhile what end there can be of ills or what limit at last is to be set to punishments, and fears lest these very evils be enhanced after death. The life of fools at length becomes a hell here on earth.

This too you may sometimes say to yourself, 'even worthy Ancus has quitted the light with his eyes, who was far far better than thou, unconscionable man. And since then many other kings and kesars have been laid low, who lorded it over mighty nations. He too, even he who erst paved a way over the great sea and made a path for his legions to march over the deep and taught them to pass on foot over the salt pools and set at naught the roarings of the sea, trampling on them with his horses, had the light taken from him and shed forth his soul from his dying body. The son of the Scipios, thunderbolt of war, terror of Carthage, yielded his bones to earth just as if he were the lowest menial. Think too of the inventors of all sciences and graceful arts, think of the

companions of the Heliconian maids; among whom Homer bore the
sceptre without a peer, and he now sleeps the same sleep as others. Then
there is Democritus, who, when a ripe old age had warned him that the
memory-waking motions of his mind were waning, by his own sponta-
neous act offered up his head to death. Even Epicurus passed away,
when his light of life had run its course, he who surpassed in intellect the
race of man and quenched the light of all, as the ethereal sun arisen
quenches the stars.' Wilt thou then hesitate and think it a hardship to
die? Thou for whom life is well nigh dead whilst yet thou livest and seest
the light, who spendest the greater part of thy time in sleep and snorest
wide awake and ceasest not to see visions and hast a mind troubled with
groundless terror and canst not discover often what it is that ails thee,
when besotted man thou art sore pressed on all sides with full many
cares and goest astray tumbling about in the wayward wanderings of thy
mind.

If, just as they are seen to feel that a load is on their mind which wears
them out with its pressure, men might apprehend from what causes too
it is produced and whence such a pile, if I may say so, of ill lies on their
breast, they would not spend their life as we see them now for the most
part do, not knowing any one of them what he means and wanting ever
change of place as though he might lay his burden down. The man who
is sick of home often issues forth from his large mansion, and as
suddenly comes back to it, finding as he does that he is no better off
abroad. He races to his country-house, driving his jennets in headlong
haste, as if hurrying to bring help to a house on fire: he yawns the
moment he has reached the door of his house, or sinks heavily into sleep
and seeks forgetfulness, or even in haste goes back again to town. In this
way each man flies from himself (but self from whom, as you may be
sure is commonly the case, he cannot escape, clings to him in his own
despite), hates too himself, because he is sick and knows not the cause of
the malady; for if he could rightly see into this, relinquishing all else
each man would study to learn the nature of things, since the point at
stake is the condition for eternity, not for one hour, in which mortals
have to pass all the time which remains for them to expect after death.

Once more what evil lust of life is this which constrains us with such
force to be so mightily troubled in doubts and dangers? A sure term of
life is fixed for mortals, and death cannot be shunned, but meet it we
must. Moreover we are ever engaged, ever involved in the same
pursuits, and no new pleasure is struck out by living on; but whilst what
we crave is wanting, it seems to transcend all the rest; then, when it has
been gotten, we crave something else, and ever does the same thirst of
life possess us, as we gape for it open-mouthed. Quite doubtful it is what

fortune the future will carry with it or what chance will bring us or what end is at hand. Nor by prolonging life do we take one tittle from the time past in death nor can we fret anything away, whereby we may haply be a less long time in the condition of the dead. Therefore you may complete as many generations as you please during your life; none the less however will that everlasting death await you; and for no less long a time will he be no more in being, who beginning with to-day has ended his life, than the man who has died many months and years ago.

ST. AUGUSTINE

from *The City of God*

Book XIII
I

On the fall of the first human beings and the mortality that it entailed.

Now that I have settled the very difficult problem respecting the rise of our present world and the beginning of the human race, I next take up in my discussion, as the logical order of my subject matter requires, the fall of the first human being, or rather human beings, and the origin and dissemination of human death. For God had not made human beings in the same way as angels, that is, incapable of dying under any circumstances, even though they should have sinned. Rather, in their case, fulfilment of their duty of obedience was to bring angelic death-lessness and an eternity of bliss with no intervening period of death, whereas disobedience would be very justly punished with death. This is a point that I have already made in the preceding book too.

II

On the death that can befall the soul, which is destined to live on somehow, and the death to which the body is subject.

But I see that I should explain somewhat more carefully what is actually meant by death. To begin with, although the human soul is correctly said to be immortal, yet it too is subject to its own sort of death. For when the soul is termed immortal, the meaning is that it does not cease to have life and feeling in some degree no matter how slight. On the other hand, when the body is termed mortal, the meaning is that it may be abandoned by life completely and has no life of its own at all. Consequently, it is the death of a soul when God abandons it, just as it is the death of a body when its soul abandons it. Hence the death of both combined, that is, of the whole human being, occurs when a soul abandoned by God abandons a body. For under these circumstances neither does the soul derive life from God nor the body life from the soul.

Moreover, death of the whole human being in this way leads to the second death, a term sanctioned by the authority of God's word. It is to this death that our Saviour referred when he said: "Fear him who has power to destroy both body and soul in hell." But since this does not happen until after the soul and body have been so closely welded that they are utterly inseparable, we may wonder how it can be said that the body is slain if in its death it is not abandoned by the soul but tormented while it is animated by a soul and possessed of feeling. In connexion with that final and everlasting punishment, a subject on which I must discourse more fully in its proper place, we can, it is true, rightly speak of the death of the soul because it derives no life from God. But how can we speak here of any death of the body since that does derive life from the soul? Indeed, the body cannot otherwise experience those physical pains that it is destined to feel after the resurrection. The answer is perhaps this: since life of any sort constitutes some good, and pain some evil, we ought not to say that a body is alive if the soul resides in it, not in order to make it live, but to make it hurt.

The soul is therefore deriving life from God when it lives a good life, for it can live a good life only if God works in it for good. The body, however, derives life from the soul when the soul lives in it, whether or not the soul itself derives life from God. For in the bodies of the irreligious life is not a life of their souls but of their bodies; and souls, even when dead, that is, when abandoned by God, can contribute life to them since their own life, no matter how slight, which is the source of their immortality, does not come to a halt. But in the punishment of the last judgement such existence may well be called death rather than life, for, although the man does not cease to have feelings, yet his feelings are neither sweetened by pleasure nor made wholesome by calm; rather, sensation is painful and thereby punitive. Moreover, it is called the second death because it comes after the first, which effects the separation of two substances that are joined, whether it be God and the soul or the soul and the body. Consequently, we may say of the first death, that of the body, that it is good for those who are good and evil for those who are evil. But as for the second death, just as it happens to no one who is good, so doubtless it is good for no one.

VI

On the evil of death in general, whereby the union of soul and body is sundered.

Wherefore, so far as the death of the body or, in other words, the separation of the soul from the body is concerned, it is not good for anyone when those who are said to be dying are undergoing it. For a grating and unnatural feeling is produced by the force itself that rends asunder the two things that were joined and interwoven in the living person; and this experience lasts until there is a complete loss of sensation, which was present precisely because of the union of soul and flesh. But all this anguish is sometimes cut short by a single blow to the body or by a sudden seizure of the soul, the swiftness of which prevents its being felt.

Yet, whatever it is in the dying that removes with a feeling of distress the power of feeling, it adds to the merit of patience when it is borne with religious faith, but it does not expunge the term 'penalty.' Thus, although death is doubtless the penalty incurred by a man at birth as a direct descendant of the first man, yet, if it is paid on behalf of religion and righteousness, it becomes the glory of a man at rebirth; and although death is recompense of sin, it sometimes succeeds in bringing it about that there is no recompense for sin.

VIII

That when the saints undergo the first death in the cause of truth they are thereby freed from the second death.

Indeed, a more careful consideration shows that, even when a person dies loyally and gloriously in the cause of truth, death is avoided. For he undergoes some part of it that he may not have the whole come to him, as well as the second, never-ending death besides. He accepts separation of soul from body to prevent separation of God from the soul before separation of soul from body; otherwise, when the first death of the entire man had run its course, it would be followed by the second death, which is eternal.

Therefore death, as I said, is not good for anyone at the time when it is experienced by the dying and is causing them to die, but it is borne gloriously in order to keep or to obtain something that is good. But when those who are described as already dead are in the state of death, there is no mistake in saying that it is evil for the evil and good for the good. For the souls of the righteous that are separated from the body are at rest, whereas those of the wicked suffer punishment; and this situation obtains until the bodies of the righteous are resurrected to an eternal life and those of the wicked to an eternal or second death.

IX

Whether the time of death, at which the feeling of life is taken away, is properly said to be when people are dying or when they are dead.

But there arises the question whether the period during which the souls, after separation from their bodies, are in either a good or a bad state is better referred to as after death or in death. If we say after death, then it is no longer death itself, which is over and past, that is good or evil, but the actual life of the soul after it. Still, death was evil for them at the time when it existed, that is, when they were experiencing it as they were dying, since the grievous, painful feeling of it was present in them; and this is an evil which the good use to good advantage. But once death is completed, how can it be good or evil if it no longer is?

Further, if we should observe still more carefully, it will become clear that not even that process which produced, as we said, a grievous and painful feeling in the dying is actually death. For as long as they experience feeling, they are certainly still alive; and if they are still alive, we must speak of them as before death rather than in death, because when death has come it takes away all the physical sensation that is so painful while death is approaching. And this is why it is difficult to explain how we can describe as dying those who are not yet dead, though, while death threatens, they are already racked in a final and fatal agony. Yet they are rightly called dying because when death, which is already imminent, has come, they are not termed dying but dead.

Accordingly, only a living person can be a dying one, for even when a man is as far gone in life as those who we say are giving up the ghost, surely he who has not yet been parted from it is still alive. The very same person then is at once both dying and living, but he is approaching death and withdrawing from life. Nevertheless, he is still in life because the soul is in his body, but not yet in death because he has not yet withdrawn from the body. But if, when he has withdrawn, he is not even then in death but rather after death, who could say when he is in death? Indeed, if no one can be at once dying and living, there will not even be anyone who is dying, since, as long as the soul is in the body, we cannot deny that he is living. Or if we must say rather that the person in whose body death is already in process of taking place is dying and if no one can be at once living and dying, then when in the world is he living?

X

Whether the life of mortals should be called death rather than life.

Indeed, from the very moment that a person begins his existence in this body that is destined to die, there is never a point when death is not coming on. For this advance of man into death is the effect of the change to which he is subject at every moment of our present life, if we can still call it life. Certainly there is no one who will not be nearer to death a year later than he was a year before or will not be tomorrow than he is today or is not today than he was yesterday or will not be a little later than he is now or is not now than he was a little while ago. And the reason for this is as follows: whatever length of time our life goes on, all this is subtracted from our whole life-span, and what is left becomes less and less each day, so that our present life is nothing but a race toward the goal of death—a race in which no one is allowed either a brief pause or the slightest slackening of pace, but all are propelled with a uniform motion and driven along with no variation in the rate of progress.

Thus the person who had a shorter life did not complete a day more quickly than he who had a longer life; rather, since both had an equal number of moments taken from them at an equal rate, one was nearer and the other farther from the goal to which they both were racing with no difference of speed. It is one thing to have traversed a longer way and quite another to have proceeded at a slower pace. Hence the person who takes more time on the way to his death does not advance with less speed but covers a greater distance.

Further, if a person begins to die, that is, to be in a state of death from the time that the process of death itself commences in him, then surely he is in a state of death from the time that he begins to exist in this body. For death is the diminution of life because, once life has been ended by diminishing, he will then be past the time of death, not in death. Indeed, what else takes place but death every single day, hour and minute until, when life is used up, death, which was going on, is complete and time, which comprised the period during death when life was being diminished, now enters upon the period after death? Accordingly, if man cannot be at one and the same time both in life and in death, he is never in life from the time he is in this body which is dying rather than living.

But perhaps man is at once both in life and in death, that is to say, he is in life, living it until it is wholly removed, but at the same time in death because he is dying from the moment that his life is diminished. For if he is not in life, what is it that suffers diminution until it is completely used up? On the other hand, if he is not in death, what is the diminution of life essentially? It is quite proper to speak of the time after death once life has been wholly removed from the body precisely because the time when life was being diminished was itself death. For if, after life has been removed, man finds himself not in death but past death, when will he be in death if not when life is being diminished?

XI

Whether anyone can at the same time be both living and dead.

On the other hand, to say that a man is already in death before he arrives at death is perhaps absurd, for what does he approach as he passes the moments of his life if he is already in death? And this would seem so especially since it is quite anomalous to speak of a person as both living and dying at the same time, inasmuch as he cannot be awake and asleep at the same time. Hence we must ask when he will be a dying man. For before death comes, he is not dying, but living. But when death has come, he will be dead, not dying. Accordingly, the former state is still prior to death, the latter already subsequent to death.

When then is he in the state of death? For that is when he is dying, and thus there are three separate states, 'living,' 'dying,' and 'dead,' corresponding, respectively, to the three stages that we speak of, 'before death,' 'in death,' and 'after death.' It is therefore very hard to define when he is dying, that is, in death, a state in which he is neither living, which is prior to death, nor dead, which is subsequent to death, but dying, that is, in death. For as long as the soul is in the body, especially if sensation is also present, man, who consists of body and soul, doubtless lives, and for this reason he must be described as still being before death, not in death. When the soul, however, has departed and removed all bodily sensation, the man is spoken of as past death and dead.

There vanishes then between these two states the interval during which a person is dying or in process of death. For if he is still living, he is before death; if he has ceased to live, he is already past death. Accordingly, he is never conceived to be dying, that is, to be in the midst of death. So too, as time goes by, we seek the present moment without finding it because there is no duration of any length in the passage from future to past.

We must surely then be careful lest, following this line of reasoning, we find ourselves saying that there is no death of the body. For if there is such a thing, when can it be? It cannot be in anyone nor can anyone be in it. If a person is alive, there is still no death because life is a state before death, not during death. On the other hand, if there has been a cessation of life, then there is no longer any death because here too is a state not during death, but after death. But, again, if there is no death before something or after something, what do we mean by the phrase 'before death' or 'after death'? For these too are meaningless expressions if there is no death. Would that we had led such a good life in paradise that there really was no death! But, as things stand, death not only exists but is so troublesome that it can neither be defined by any mode of speech nor be avoided by any device.

Let us then follow common usage in our speech, as indeed we ought, and say 'before death' for the time before death occurs, just as we read in Scripture: "Praise no man before his death." Let us also say, when it has occurred: "Such and such happened after the death of so and so." Let us speak too as best we can of contemporary time, as when, for example, we express ourselves thus: "Dying, he made his will," and: "Dying, he bequeathed such and such to so and so." And yet, unless he had been living, he could not have done this at all; in fact, he did it rather before death, not in death.

Let us speak also in the same terms as the holy Scriptures, which do not scruple to say that the dead too are not past death but in death. Hence indeed comes the statement: "Since there is none in death who is mindful of thee." For until they are brought to life again, they are rightly said to be in death, just as every one is said to be in slumber until he wakes up. Still, although we say that those who lie in slumber are sleeping, we cannot similarly say that those who are already dead are dying. For those who are already separated from their bodies are not still dying. These remarks, of course, concern only the death of the body, which is the subject of our present discussion.

But this is what I said could not be defined by any mode of speech. How can either those who are dying be said to be living or those who are already dead be said, even after death, to be still in death? For how can they be regarded as after death if they are still in death, especially since we do not say that they are dying then either, as we say that those who are in slumber are sleeping and those who are in weariness are weary and those who are in pain are surely suffering pain and those who are in life are living? But the dead, until they rise again, are said to be in death and yet the term 'dying' cannot be used of them.

Hence I think that it is neither improper nor discordant that it has come about, though not by human effort, yet perhaps by divine ordinance, that neither were the grammarians able to conjugate in Latin the verb *moritur* ('he dies') according to the same rule as the other verbs of this type. For from the verb *oritur* ('he arises') comes the past tense *ortus est* ('he has arisen'), and all like verbs are conjugated with perfect participles. But if we ask for the past tense of the verb *moritur*, the regular answer is *mortuus est* ('he has died' or 'he is dead'), the letter *u* being doubled. For *mortuus* is used in the same way as *fatuus* ('foolish'), *arduus* ('steep'), *conspicuus* ('visible'), and any like words that do not imply past time, but, being adjectives, are declined without distinction of tense. That adjective, moreover, is employed in place of a past participle as if to make a tense where none can be. The result of this is, appropriately enough, that the verb itself can no more be declined by us in speech than can the act that it denotes in reality.

Yet with the help of the grace of our Redeemer we may be enabled to decline, that is, evade, at least the second death. For the death that is effected, not by the separation of soul and body, but rather by the union of both for eternal punishment is more serious and the worst of all evils. There, conversely, men will not be in a state before death or after death but always in death, and for this reason never living, never dead, but endlessly dying. Indeed, man will never be worse off in death than where death itself will be deathless.

XII

On the death with which God threatened the first human beings if they should violate his commandment.

To the question then what kind of death it was with which God threatened the first human beings if they should violate the commandment received from him and should not observe obedience, whether it was death of the soul or of the body or of the whole man, or that which is called the second death, we must answer: "All of them." For the first death consists of two deaths, total death of all of them. Just as the whole earth consists of many lands and the whole church of many churches, so total death consists of all deaths.

The reason for this is as follows: the first death consists of two deaths, one of the soul and the other of the body, and thus the first death is that of the whole man when the soul without God and without the body suffers punishment for a certain length of time; the second death, on the other hand, occurs when the soul without God suffers eternal punishment along with the body. Accordingly, when God said concerning the forbidden food to that first man whom he had placed in paradise: "In the day that you eat of it you shall die," his threat embraced not only the first part of the first death, when the soul is deprived of God, nor only the second part, when the body is deprived of the soul, nor even the entire first death alone, when the soul undergoes punishment after it is separated from both God and the body, but it included every kind of death down to the very last, which is called the second death and is followed by no other.

XVI

On the philosophers who do not think that the separation of soul from body is a punishment, although Plato represents the supreme God as assuring the lesser deities that they are never to be stripped of their bodies.

But the philosophers, against whose slanders we are defending the City of God, that is to say, his church, are wise in their own eyes when they scoff at our statement that the separation of soul from body should be accounted among its punishments. The reason for this is that they hold that the soul attains its fullest bliss in the moment when, utterly stripped of all body, it returns to God simple, alone and, in a sense, naked.

In this matter, if I found nothing in their writings to refute this belief, I should have to argue more painstakingly to demonstrate that it is not the body as such but a corruptible body that is burdensome to the soul. This is what lies behind the following statement that we quoted in the preceding book from our Scriptures: "For the corruptible body is heavy upon the soul." Surely, by adding 'corruptible' the sage meant that the soul was weighed down, not by just any sort of body, but by the body such as it became as a result of sin and consequent punishment. And even if he had not added this term, we ought not to have understood anything else. But Plato declares in the clearest manner that the deities, who were made by the supreme God, have immortal bodies, and he represents God himself, their maker, as promising them a great boon in that they will for ever remain united to their bodies and never be severed from them by any death. Now, in view of all this, why is it that those philosophers, seeking to harry the Christian faith, pretend not to know what they do know or even prefer to be at odds with themselves and to speak against themselves, if only they may contradict us unremittingly?

Here are the very words of Plato himself, as translated by Cicero into Latin, in which he presents the supreme God addressing the deities whom he made and saying: "You who have sprung from the stock of the gods, give heed. The works of which I am parent and author are exempt from dissolution against my will, although everything that is fastened together can be sundered; but it is nowise good to choose to undo what is bound together by reason. But since you have had a beginning, you cannot be immortal and indestructible. Yet you will by no means be destroyed, nor will any necessity of death annihilate you or be more powerful than my purpose, which serves as a stronger bond for your continued existence than those bonds by which you were fastened together [at the time that you were created]." Thus Plato says both that the gods are mortal because of the union of body and soul and that they are yet immortal because of the will and purpose of God who made them.

If then it is punishment for the soul to be bound up in any sort of body, why is it that God addresses them as though they were anxious for fear that they may die, that is, be detached from the body, and why does he give them assurance of their immortality? This assurance, moreover, is based, not on their nature, which is composite rather than simple, but on his own unconquerable will, by which he has power to preserve such things as have a beginning from perishing and such as have been joined together from coming apart, and to make them endure without deterioration.

But whether these words of Plato in reference to the stars are true is another question. For it does not follow that we must grant him that those luminous globes or little disks that shine with physical light over the lands whether by day or by night are animated by souls of their own and that these souls are endowed with understanding and happiness. He emphatically makes this same statement about the universe as a whole, speaking of it as a single living thing of the greatest size that encloses all other living things. But, as I said, this is another question, which I have not undertaken to discuss at the moment.

I have thought it best to bring up just this one point against those who plume themselves on being called or being Platonists and whose pride in this name makes them ashamed to be Christians. They fear that, if they share one designation with the common mass, it will detract for the wearers of the Greek cloak from the prestige of their fewness, for they are puffed up in inverse proportion to their number. And so in their quest for something to censure in Christian doctrine they rail at the immortality of the body, as if there were any inconsistency in our seeking happiness for the soul and at the same time requiring it to exist for ever in a body, as if the bonds that bind them must be vexatious. Yet it is their founder and teacher Plato who says that the supreme God granted to the deities who were made by him the boon of never dying, that is, of never being separated from the bodies to which he joined them.

XVII

Against those who maintain that earthly bodies cannot become imperishable and eternal.

These philosophers also argue that earthly bodies cannot be everlasting, although they do not doubt that the entire earth itself constitutes a central and everlasting member of their god; by god they mean not the supreme God, but the great god that this whole universe is to them. Well then, the supreme God created for them what they regard as another god, that is, this universe, with precedence over the other deities that are below him. Moreover, they think that this god is animate, possessing, that is, a soul which is, so they say, rational or intelligent and shut up within that massive body. Further, according to them, God established the four elements like physical members of that same body, placed and arranged in their proper places; and to secure this great god of theirs from ever dying they would have it that the union of these elements is indissoluble and everlasting. Granted all this, what reason is there, if the earth or central member, as it were, in the body of the larger animate being is eternal, why the bodies of other animate beings belonging to earth cannot be eternal if God were to will this as well as that?

Their contention is that earth, the source of the earthly bodies of living things, must be returned to earth; this, they say, is why these bodies must break up and perish and thus be restored to the steadfast and eternal earth from which they were derived. But suppose that a person made a similar assertion about fire and said that the bodies taken up from the universal fire for the creation of heavenly beings must be returned to it. On this hypothesis, will not the immortality which Plato, speaking in the person of the supreme God, promised to such gods be rescinded by the violence, so to speak, of this line of argument? Or is this impossible in that region because God, whose will, as Plato says, no force can conquer, does not will it? What then is there to prevent God from having power to bring about the same thing in the case of earthly bodies too, especially since Plato acknowledges God's power to bring it about that what has a beginning need not perish nor need what has been bound come apart nor what has been taken from the elements be returned, and that souls established in bodies may not only never forsake them but even enjoy immortality and everlasting happiness together with them?

Why then should God not have power to bring it about that earthly things may not perish either? Is it that his power does not extend so far as Christians believe, but only so far as the Platonists hold? Those philosophers no doubt were in a position to know the purpose and power of God, whereas the prophets were not! No, quite the contrary; it was the prophets of God who were taught by his Spirit that they might reveal his will to the extent that he saw fit, while the philosophers were misled by human conjecture when they sought to discover it.

But neither ignorance nor obstinacy should have induced these philosophers to make such a mistake as to plead against themselves so patently. Yet this is what they do. On the one hand, they maintain with great force of argument that the soul, in order to be happy, must keep clear not only of an earthly body but of every kind of body, and, on the other hand, they declare that the gods have souls which are supremely happy and yet bound up with eternal bodies, that is, celestial souls which are bound up with bodies of fire, while the soul of Jupiter himself, whom they identify with the universe, is wholly contained in the sum total of material elements that constitute the entire structure which extends from earth to heaven.

Plato holds the view that this soul of Jupiter spreads and extends by musical ratios from the earth's innermost core or centre, as it is called by geometricians, through all its parts to the highest and furthest reaches of heaven. And thus, according to him, this universe is an everlasting living thing of the greatest magnitude and happiness; for its soul possesses the perfect bliss of wisdom and does not abandon its own body, while the body is for ever animated by the soul and, although it is not simple but composed of so many large bodies, has no power to make the soul sluggish or slothful.

Therefore, since these philosophers allow so much to their own speculations, why are they unwilling to believe that God's will and power can make earthly bodies immortal and that souls can live everlastingly and happily in them, inseparable from them by any death and undepressed by their weight? After all, they do maintain that such a life is possible for their gods in bodies of fire and for Jupiter himself, king of the gods, in the whole mass of material elements. For if a soul must shun every kind of body to be happy, let their gods flee from the starry globes and let their Jupiter flee from heaven and earth; or if they cannot do so, then let the verdict be that they are unhappy.

But these philosophers allow neither alternative, for they dare not attribute to their gods either a separation from bodies, lest they be found to worship gods who are but mortal, or a negation of bliss, lest it be shown by their own admission that their gods are unhappy. Accordingly, all bodies need not be shunned in order to attain bliss, but only such as are corruptible and vexatious, burdensome and moribund, that is, not such bodies as the bounty of God created for the first human beings, but such as penalty for sin forced upon them.

XVIII

On earthly bodies, which, according to the philosophers, cannot exist in the heavenly region because anything earthly is drawn back to earth by its natural weight.

But earthly bodies, these philosophers say, must either be held fast on earth or be forced earthward by their natural weight; and for that reason they cannot exist in heaven. Those first human beings, it is true, did live on earth, which abounded in woods and fruit and received the name 'paradise' or park. We must, however, find a reply to this argument to account for the body with which Christ ascended into heaven or for the sort of body that saints are destined to have at resurrection. Let them therefore consider a little more closely this matter of the earthly weights in themselves.

Well now, we know that human skill can take metals that immediately sink when placed in water and fashion them by certain methods into vessels that are even capable of floating. How much more credible, how much more effective must God's skill be, working in some mysterious way! His almighty will, according to Plato, preserves both things that had a beginning from perishing and things that were bound together from disintegrating. Moreover, immaterial entities are much more marvellously joined to material things than bodies are with bodies of any sort whatsoever. Surely then God can not only prevent earthly masses from being attracted to the lowest region by any weight but also enable the souls themselves to dwell in the most perfect bliss with bodies which, though earthly, yet are also incorruptible and to set these bodies wherever they wish and move them wherever they wish with the utmost ease, be it of placement or movement.

Or if angels can do this and carry off any earthly animals they please from wherever they please and set them down wherever they please, are we really to believe that they cannot do this without feeling the weight of the burdens? If not, then why should we not believe that the spirits of the saints, made perfect and happy by divine dispensation, can without any difficulty transport their bodies wherever they wish and set them wherever they wish? For granted that earthly bodies, like burdens whose weight we normally feel when we carry them, have their weight proportional to their mass, and thus the weight of a greater bodily mass is more oppressive than that of a smaller mass, nevertheless, the soul finds the organs of its flesh lighter to carry when they are sound and sturdy than when they are feeble and shrunken. And although a sound and healthy person is heavier for others to carry than a thin and sickly one, yet the person himself can move and carry his body with greater agility when he enjoys good health and has more weight than when through plague or starvation he has very little strength. Thus even when we have our earthly bodies, although they are still subject to putrefaction and death, it is not the weight of their mass, but the state of their constitution that makes all the difference. And who can find words to express the vast difference between the so-called health of our present state and the immortality of our future condition?

Our creed then is not refuted by the philosophers' argument about the weight of bodies. Now I will not put the question why they refuse to believe that there can be an earthly body in heaven, when the entire earth is balanced upon nothing. For perhaps an even more probable argument against our view may be drawn from the very existence of a centre of the universe and from the fact that all heavier bodies converge upon it. What I do say is this: Let us suppose that the lesser gods, who were charged by Plato with the creation of man as well as of the other terrestrial animals, were able, as he declares, to remove from fire the property of burning, while leaving that of brightness to flash through the eyes. If then the will and power of the supreme God can, as Plato himself has allowed, preserve both things that had a beginning from perishing and the union of things so different and unlike as material and immaterial substances from the possibility of being parted by any means of disintegration, shall we hesitate to allow him to abolish putrefaction of the flesh of any man on whom he bestows immortality, while leaving its properties intact, and to retain the harmony of design among its members, while removing the sluggishness of its weight? But I intend to discuss both our belief in the resurrection of the dead and the immortality of their bodies more fully, God willing, at the end of this work.

XIX

Against the views of those who do not believe that the first human beings would have been immortal if they had not sinned, but hold that the everlasting existence of souls is incorporeal.

Let us now resume our discussion about the bodies of the first human beings, for they could not have fallen victim even to that death which is said to be good for the good and which is known not only to the few that have understanding or faith but to all, had it not come as a just recompense in consequence of sin; this is the death by which the separation of the soul from the body is effected and through which without question the body of a living being, which was visibly alive, visibly perishes. True, there can be no doubt that the souls of the just and holy who are deceased live in repose. Yet they would be so much better off living with their bodies in sound health that even those who think it perfect bliss to be completely disembodied refute their own belief by a conflicting tenet.

None of them will venture to rate wise men, whether yet to die or already dead (that is, men who either already are bodiless or presently will abandon their bodies) higher than the immortal gods to whom the supreme God, according to Plato, promises the immense privilege of an indissoluble life or, in other words, an everlasting union with their bodies. But Plato also thinks that men, provided they have lived holy and just lives here on earth, receive the best reward that can be when they are separated from their bodies and received into the bosom of the very gods who never leave their bodies,

> That, all forgetting, they may seek the vault
> On high again, and soon begin to have
> A will once more in bodies to reside,

as Virgil so admirably expressed this view derived from Plato's creed.

Thus Plato does not believe that the souls of mortals can always remain in their bodies, but rather that they are released by an inevitable death. Nor does he think that these souls survive for ever without bodies; rather people live and die in ceaseless alternation as they pass from one state to the other. Yet there seems to be a distinction between the fate of wise men and that of the rest of mankind. For, according to him, after death the former are borne to the starry heavens, and each of them reposes for a somewhat longer time on the star appropriate for him. From that star again, when he has forgotten his old misery and yielded to the desire for embodiment, he returns to the toils and troubles of mortals. On the other hand, those who have led stupid lives start on the cycle once more after a very short interval, occupying bodies, whether of man or beast, that are assigned to each according to his desert.

This then is the exceedingly harsh fate to which Plato consigned even good and wise souls, for they were not provided with bodies with which they could live for ever free from death. This meant that they could neither occupy their bodies permanently nor survive without them in everlasting purity. As I have already said in a preceding book, this Platonic tenet caused Porphyry embarrassment in the Christian era; he not only banned the bodies of beasts from union with human souls but also held that the souls of wise men were so completely released from the bonds of the body that they abandoned every sort of body and were preserved for ever happy in the Father's presence. Thus it was that, not to seem outdone by Christ, who promised an everlasting life to saints, Porphyry too assigned purified souls to a place of everlasting happiness without any return to former misery. On the other hand, in order also to oppose Christ, he denied the resurrection of incorruptible bodies and maintained that souls would live for ever not only without earthly bodies but without any bodies at all.

Yet, despite this belief, such as it was, Porphyry did not go so far as to teach also that these souls should not pay pious homage to gods with bodies. Why so, unless because he did not believe that these souls, although they were accompanied by no body, were superior to those gods? Therefore, if those philosophers will not venture, as I do not think they will, to rank human souls above gods who are supremely happy and yet endowed with everlasting bodies, why do they consider the message of Christianity so absurd, when it declares that the first human beings too were so created that, had they not sinned, no death would have parted them from their bodies? Rather they would have received as a reward for maintaining obedience the gift of immortality and would have lived joined to their bodies for ever. Moreover, the saints will possess at resurrection those very bodies in which they toiled in this life; and their bodies will be such that neither shall any deterioration or handicap affect their flesh nor any grief or misfortune their bliss.

SEXTUS EMPIRICUS

from Outlines of Pyrrhonism

A similar account may be given of reverence toward the departed. Some wrap the dead up completely and then cover them with earth, thinking that it is impious to expose them to the sun; but the Egyptians take out their entrails and embalm them and keep them above ground with themselves. The fish-eating tribes of the Ethiopians cast them into the lakes, there to be devoured by the fish; the Hyrcanians expose them as a prey to dogs, and some of the Indians to vultures. And they say that some of the Troglodytes take the corpse to a hill, and then after tying its head to its feet cast stones upon it amidst laughter, and when they have made a heap of stones over it they leave it there. And some of the barbarians slay and eat those who are over sixty years old, but bury in the earth those who die young. Some burn the dead; and of these some recover and preserve their bones, while others show no care but leave them scattered about. And they say that the Persians impale their dead and embalm them with nitre, after which they wrap them round in bandages. How much grief others endure for the dead we see ourselves.

Some, too, believe death itself to be dreadful and horrible, others do not. Thus Euripides says:

Who knows if life be but the state of death,
And death be counted life in realms below?[1]

And Epicurus declares: "Death is nothing to us; for what is dissolved is senseless, and what is senseless is nothing to us." They also declare that, inasmuch as we are compounded of soul and body, and death is a dissolution of soul and body, when we exist death does not exist (for we are not being dissolved), and when death exists we do not exist, for through the cessation of the compound of soul and body we too cease to exist. And Heraclitus states that both life and death exist both in our state of life and in our state of death; for when we live our souls are dead and buried within us, and when we die our souls revive and live. And some even suppose that dying is better for us than living. Thus Euripides says:

> Rather should we assemble to bewail
> The babe new-born, such ills has he to face;
> Whereas the dead, who has surcease from woe,
> With joy and gladness we should bear from home.[2]

These lines, too, spring from the same sentiment:

> Not to have been begotten at all were the best thing for mortals,
>   Nor to have looked upon fiery rays of the sun:
> Or, if begotten, to hasten amain to the portals of Hades,
>   And to lie unmoved robed in masses of earth.[3]

We know, too, the facts about Cleobis and Biton which Herodotus relates in his story of the Argive priestess.[4] It is reported, also, that some of the Thracians sit around the new-born babe and chant dirges. So, then, death should not be considered a thing naturally dreadful, just as life should not be considered a thing naturally good. Thus none of the things mentioned above is naturally of this character or of that, but all are matters of convention and relative.

1. Euripides, *Frag.* 638.
2. Euripides, *Frag.* 449.
3. Theognis 425 ff.
4. Their mother Cydippe (the "Argive priestess" of Hera) prayed to the goddess to grant her sons Cleobis and Biton the best boons for mortals. The same night both died in their sleep. Cf. Herodotus, i. 31.

MICHEL DE MONTAIGNE

That to Philosophize is to Learn to Die

Cicero says that to philosophize is nothing else but to prepare for death. This is because study and contemplation draw our soul out of us to some extent and keep it busy outside the body; which is a sort of apprenticeship and semblance of death. Or else it is because all the wisdom and reasoning in the world boils down finally to this point: to teach us not to be afraid to die. In truth, either reason is a mockery, or it must aim solely at our contentment, and the sum of its labors must tend to make us live well and at our ease, as Holy Scripture says. All the opinions in the world agree on this—that pleasure is our goal—though they choose different means to it. Otherwise they would be thrown out right away; for who would listen to a man who would set up our pain and discomfort as his goal?

The dissensions of the philosophic sects in this matter are merely verbal. *Let us skip over such frivolous subtleties* [Seneca]. There is more stubbornness and wrangling than befits such a sacred profession. But whatever role man undertakes to play, he always plays his own at the same time. Whatever they say, in virtue itself the ultimate goal we aim at is voluptuousness. I like to beat their ears with that word, which so goes against their grain. And if it means a certain supreme pleasure and excessive contentment, this is due more to the assistance of virtue than to any other assistance. This voluptuousness, for being more lusty, sinewy, robust, and manly, is only the more seriously voluptuous. And we should have given virtue the name of pleasure, a name more favorable, sweet, and natural; not that of vigor, as we have named it. That other baser sort of voluptuousness, if it deserved that beautiful name, should have acquired it in competition, not as a privilege. I find it less free of inconveniences and obstacles than virtue. Besides the fact that its enjoyment is more momentary, watery, and weak, it has its vigils, its fasts, and its hardships, its sweat and blood; and, more particularly, its poignant sufferings of so many kinds, and an accompanying satiety so heavy that it is the equivalent of penance. We are very wrong to suppose that these disadvantages act as a spur and a spice to its sweetness, as in nature a thing is enlivened by its opposite, and to say, when we come to virtue, that similar consequences and difficulties oppress it, make it austere and inaccessible; whereas, much more than in the case of voluptuousness, they ennoble, whet, and heighten the divine and perfect pleasure that virtue affords us. That man is surely very unworthy of its acquaintance who balances its cost against its fruits; he knows neither its graces nor its use. Those who go on teaching us that the quest of it is rugged and laborious, though the enjoyment of it is agreeable, what are they doing but telling us that it is always disagreeable? For what human means ever attained the enjoyment of virtue? The most perfect have been quite content to aspire to it and to approach it, without possessing it. But those others are wrong; since in all the pleasures that we know, even the pursuit is pleasant. The attempt is made fragrant by the quality of the thing it aims at, for it is a good part of the effect, and consubstantial with it. The happiness and blessedness that shines in virtue fills all its appurtenances and approaches even to the first entrance and the utmost barrier.

Now among the principal benefits of virtue is disdain for death, a means that furnishes our life with a soft tranquillity and gives us a pure and pleasant enjoyment of it, without which all other pleasures are extinguished. That is why all rules meet and agree at this point. And though they all with one accord lead us also to scorn pain, poverty, and other accidents to which human life is subject, it is not with equal insistence; partly because these accidents are not so inevitable (most men spend their life without tasting poverty, and some also without feeling pain and illness, like Xenophilus the musician, who lived a hundred and six years in complete health), and also because at worst, whenever we please, death can put an end, and deny access, to all our other woes. But as for death itself, it is inevitable.

> We are all forced down the same road. Our fate,
> Tossed in the urn, will spring out soon or late,
> And force us helpless into Charon's bark,
> Passengers destined for eternal dark.
>
> HORACE

And consequently, if it frightens us, it is a continual source of torment which cannot be alleviated at all. There is no place from which it may not come to us; we may turn our heads constantly this way and that as in a suspicious country: *death always hangs over us, like the stone over Tantalus* [Cicero]. Our law courts often send criminals to be executed at the place where the crime was committed. On the way, take them past beautiful houses, give them as good a time as you like—

> Not even a Siclian feast
> Can now produce for him a pleasant taste,
> Nor song of birds, nor music of the lyre
> Restore his sleep
>
> HORACE

—do you think that they can rejoice in these things, and that the final purpose of their trip, being steadily before their eyes, will not have changed and spoiled their taste for all these pleasures?

> He hears it as it comes, counts days, measures the breath
> Of life upon their length, tortured by coming death.
>
> CLAUDIAN

The goal of our career is death. It is the necessary object of our aim. If it frightens us, how is it possible to go a step forward without feverishness? The remedy of the common herd is not to think about it. But from what brutish stupidity can come so gross a blindness! They have to bridle the ass by the tail,

Who sets his mind on moving only backward.

LUCRETIUS

It is no wonder they are so often caught in the trap. These people take fright at the mere mention of death, and most of them cross themselves at that name, as at the name of the devil. And because death is mentioned in wills, don't expect them to set about writing a will until the doctor has given them their final sentence; and then, between the pain and the fright, Lord knows with what fine judgment they will concoct it.

Because this syllable struck their ears too harshly and seemed to them unlucky, the Romans learned to soften it or to spread it out into a periphrasis. Instead of saying "He is dead," they say "He has ceased to live," "He has lived." Provided it is life, even past life, they take comfort. We have borrowed from them our "late Mr. John."

Perhaps it is true that, as the saying goes, the delay is worth the money. I was born between eleven o'clock and noon on the last day of February, 1533, as we reckon time now, beginning the year in January. It was only just two weeks ago that I passed the age of thirty-nine years, and I need at least that many more; but to be bothered meanwhile by the thought of a thing so far off would be folly. After all, young and old leave life on the same terms. None goes out of it otherwise than as if he had just entered it. And besides, there is no man so decrepit that as long as he sees Methuselah ahead of him, he does not think he has another twenty years left in his body. Furthermore, poor fool that you are, who has assured you the term of your life? You are building on the tales of doctors. Look rather at facts and experience. By the ordinary run of things, you have been living a long time now by extraordinary favor. You have passed the accustomed limits of life. And to prove this, count how many more of your acquaintances have died before your age than have attained it. And even for those who have glorified their lives by renown, make a list, and I'll wager I'll find more of them who died before thirty-five than after. It is completely reasonable and pious to take our example from the humanity of Jesus Christ himself; now he finished his life at thirty-three. The greatest man that was simply a man, Alexander, also died at that age. How many ways has death to surprise us!

Man never can plan fully to avoid
What any hour may bring.

HORACE

I leave aside fevers and pleurisies. Who would ever have thought that a duke of Brittany would be stifled to death by a crowd, as that duke was at the entrance of Pope Clement, my neighbor, into Lyons? Haven't you seen one of our kings killed at play? And did not one of his ancestors died from the charge of a hog? Aeschylus, threatened with the fall of a house, takes every precaution—in vain: he gets himself killed by a sort of roof, the shell of a tortoise dropped by a flying eagle. Another dies from a grape seed; an emperor from the scratch of a comb, while combing his hair; Aemilius Lepidus through stumbling against his theshold, and Aufidius through bumping against the door of the council chamber on his way in; and between women's thighs, Cornelius Gallus the praetor, Tigillinus, captain of the watch at Rome, Ludovico, son of Guido de Gonzaga, marquis of Mantua—and still worse, the Platonic philosopher Speusippus, and one of our Popes. Poor Bebius, a judge, in the act of granting a week's postponement to a litigant, has a seizure, his own term of living having expired; and Caius Julius, a doctor, is anointing the eyes of a patient, when along comes death and closes his. And, if I must bring myself into this, a brother of mine, Captain Saint-Martin, twenty-three years old, who had already given pretty good proof of his valor, while playing tennis was struck by a ball a little above the right ear, with no sign of contusion or wound. He did not sit down or rest, but five or six hours later he died of an apoplexy that this blow gave him. With such frequent and ordinary examples passing before our eyes, how can we possibly rid ourselves of the thought of death and of the idea that at every moment it is gripping us by the throat?

What does it matter, you will tell me, how it happens, provided we do not worry about it? I am of that opinion; and in whatever way we can put ourselves in shelter from blows, even under a calf's skin, I am not the man to shrink from it. For it is enough for me to spend my life comfortably; and the best game I can give my self I'll take, though it be as little glorious and exemplary as you like:

If but my faults could trick and please
My wits, I'd rather seem a fool at ease,
Than to be wise and rage.

HORACE

But it is folly to expect to get there that way. They go, they come, they trot, they dance—of death no news. All that is fine. But when it comes, either to them or to their wives, children, or friends, surprising them unprepared and defenseless, what torments, what cries, what frenzy, what despair overwhelms them! Did you ever see anything so dejected, so changed, so upset? We must provide for this earlier; and this brutish nonchalance, even if it could lodge in the head of a man of understanding—which I consider entirely impossible—sells us its wares too dear. If it were an enemy we could avoid, I would advise us to borrow the arms of cowardice. But since that cannot be, since it catches you just the same, whether you flee like a coward or act like a man—

> As surely it pursues the man that flees,
> Nor does it spare the haunches slack
> Of warless youth, or its timid back.

HORACE

—and since no kind of armor protects you—

> Hide as he will, cautious, in steel and brass,
> Still death will drag his head outside at last

PROPERTIUS

—let us learn to meet it steadfastly and to combat it. And to begin to strip it of its greatest advantage against us, let us take an entirely different way from the usual one. Let us rid it of its strangeness, come to know it, get used to it. Let us have nothing on our minds as often as death. At every moment let us picture it in our imagination in all its aspects. At the stumbling of a horse, the fall of a tile, the slightest pin prick, let us promptly chew on this: Well, what if it were death itself? And thereupon let us tense ourselves and make an effort. Amid feasting and gaiety let us ever keep in mind this refrain, the memory of our condition; and let us never allow ourselves to be so carried away by pleasure that we do not sometimes remember in how many ways this happiness of ours is a prey to death, and how death's clutches threaten it. Thus did the Egyptians, who, in the midst of their feasts and their greatest pleasures, had the skeleton of a dead man brought before them, to serve as a reminder to the guests.

> Look on each day as if it were your last,
> And each unlooked-for hour will seem a boon.

HORACE

It is uncertain where death awaits us; let us await it everywhere. Premeditation of death is premeditation of freedom. He who has learned how to die has unlearned how to be a slave. Knowing how to die frees us from all subjection and constraint. There is nothing evil in life for the man who has thoroughly grasped the fact that to be deprived of life is not an evil. Aemilius Paulus replied to the messenger sent by that miserable king of Macedon, his prisoner, to beg him not to lead him in his triumph: "Let him make that request of himself."

In truth, in all things, unless nature lends a hand, it is hard for art and industry to get very far. I am by nature not melancholy, but dreamy. Since my earliest days, there is nothing with which I have occupied my mind more than with images of death. Even in the most licentious season of my life,

When blooming youth enjoyed a gladsome spring,

CATULLUS

amid ladies and games, someone would think me involved in digesting some jealousy by myself, or the uncertainty of some hope, while I was thinking about I don't remember whom, who had been overtaken a few days before by a hot fever and by death, on leaving a similar feast, his head full of idleness, love, and a good time, like myself; and thinking that the same chance was hanging from my ear:

And soon it will have been, past any man's recall.

LUCRETIUS

I did not wrinkle my forehead any more over that thought than any other. It is impossible that we should fail to feel the sting of such notions at first. But by handling them and going over them, in the long run we tame them beyond question. Otherwise for my part I should be in continual fright and frenzy; for never did a man so distrust his life, never did a man set less faith in his duration. Neither does health, which thus far I have enjoyed in great vigor and with little interruption, lengthen my hope of life, nor do illnesses shorten it. Every minute I seem to be slipping away from myself. And I constantly sing myself this refrain: Whatever can be done another day can be done today. Truly risks and dangers bring us little or no nearer our end; and if we think how many million accidents remain hanging over our heads, not to mention this one that seems to threaten us most, we shall conclude that lusty or feverish, on sea or in our houses, in battle or in rest, death is equally near us. *No man is frailer than another, no man more certain of the morrow* [Seneca]. To finish what I have to do before I die, even if it were one hour's work, any leisure seems short to me.

Someone, looking through my tablets the other day, found a memorandum about something I wanted done after my death. I told him what was true, that although only a league away from my house, and hale and hearty, I had hastened to write it there, since I could not be certain of reaching home. Since I am constantly brooding over my thoughts and settling them within me, I am at all times about as well prepared as I can be. And the coming of death will teach me nothing new.

We must be always booted and ready to go, so far as it is in our power, and take especial care to have only ourselves to deal with then:

Why aim so stoutly at so many things
In our short life?

HORACE

For we shall have enough trouble without adding any. One man complains not so much of death as that it interrupts the course of a glorious victory; another, that he must move out before he has married off his daughter or supervised the education of his children; one laments losing the company of his wife, another of his son, as the principal comforts of his life.

I am at this moment in such a condition, thank God, that I can move out when he chooses, without regret for anything at all, unless for life, if I find that the loss of it weighs on me. I unbind myself on all sides; my farewells are already half made to everyone except myself. Never did a man prepare to leave the world more utterly and completely, nor detach himself from it more universally, than I propose to do.

"Wretch that I am," they say, "one all-destroying day
Takes every last reward of all my life away!"

LUCRETIUS

And the builder says:

The works remain suspended,
And the high looming walls.

VIRGIL

We must not plan anything that takes so long, or at least not with the idea of flying into a passion if we cannot see it accomplished.

We are born to act:

When death comes, let it find me at my work.

OVID

I want a man to act, and to prolong the functions of life as long as he can; and I want death to find me planting my cabbages, but careless of death, and still more of my unfinished garden. I saw a man die who, in his last extremity, complained constantly that destiny was cutting short the history, on which he was at work, of the fifteenth or sixteenth of our kings.

But this they fail to add: that after you expire
Not one of all these things will fill you with desire.

LUCRETIUS

We must rid ourselves of these vulgar and harmful humors. Just as we plant our cemeteries next to churches, and in the most frequented parts of town, in order (says Lycurgus) to accustom the common people, women and children, not to grow panicky at the sight of a dead man, and so that the constant sight of bones, tombs, and funeral processions should remind us of our condition—

> To feasts, it once was thought, slaughter lent added charms,
> Mingling with foods the sight of combatants in arms,
> And gladiators fell amid the cups, to pour
> Onto the very tables their abundant gore
>
> SILIUS ITALICUS

—and as the Egyptians, after their feasts, had a large image of death shown to the guests by a man who called out to them: "Drink and be merry, for when you are dead you will be like this"; so I have formed the habit of having death continually present, not merely in my imagination, but in my mouth. And there is nothing that I investigate so eagerly as the death of men: what words, what look, what bearing they maintained at that time; nor is there a place in the histories that I note so attentively. This shows in the abundance of my illustrative examples; I have indeed a particular fondness for this subject. If I were a maker of books, I would make a register, with comments, of various deaths. He who would teach men to die would teach them to live. Dicaearchus made a book with such a title, but with a different and less useful purpose.

People will tell me that the reality of death so far exceeds the image we form of it that, when a man is faced with it, even the most skillful fencing will do him no good. Let them talk; beyond question forethought is a great advantage. And then, is it nothing to go at least that far without disturbance and fever? What is more, Nature herself lends us her hand and gives us courage. If it is a quick and violent death, we have no leisure to fear it; if it is otherwise, I notice that in proportion as I sink into sickness, I naturally enter into a certain disdain for life. I find that I have much more trouble digesting this resolution to die when I am in health than when I have a fever. Inasmuch as I no longer cling so hard to the good things of life when I begin to lose the use and pleasure of them, I come to view death with much less frightened eyes. This makes me hope that the farther I get from life and the nearer to death, the more easily I shall accept the exchange. Even as I have experienced in many other occasions what Caesar says, that things often appear greater to us from a distance than near, so I have found that when I was healthy I had a much greater horror of sicknesses than when I felt them. The good spirits, pleasure, and strength I now enjoy make the other state appear to me so disproportionate to this one, that by imagination I magnify those inconveniences by half, and think of them as much heavier than I find they are when I have them on my shoulders. I hope I shall have the same experience with death.

Let us see how, in those ordinary changes and declines that we suffer, nature hides from us the sense of our loss and decay. What has an old man left of the vigor of his youth, and of his past life?

Alas! how scant a share of life the old have left!

MAXIMIANUS

Caesar, observing the decrepit appearance of a soldier of his guard, an exhausted and broken man, who came to him in the street to ask leave to kill himself, replied humorously: "So you think you're alive." If we fell into such a change suddenly, I don't think we could endure it. But, when we are led by Nature's hand down a gentle and virtually imperceptible slope, bit by bit, one step at a time, she rolls us into this wretched state and makes us familiar with it; so that we feel no shock when youth dies within us, which in essence and in truth is a harder death than the complete death of a languishing life or the death of old age; inasmuch as the leap is not so cruel from a painful life to no life as from a sweet and flourishing life to a grievous and painful one.

The body, when bent and bowed, has less strength to support a burden, and so has the soul; we must raise and straighten her against the assault of this adversary. For as it is impossible for the soul to be at rest while she fears death, so, if she can gain assurance against it, she can boast of a thing as it were beyond man's estate: that it is impossible for worry, torment, fear, or even the slightest displeasure to dwell in her:

The fierce look of a tyrant brings no fright
To his firm mind, nor yet the south wind's might,
That drives the Adriatic on command,
Nor Jupiter's great thunder-hurling hand.

HORACE

She is made mistress of her passions and lusts, mistress over indigence, shame, poverty, and all other wounds of fortune. Let us gain this advantage, those of us who can; this is the true and sovereign liberty, which enables us to thumb our noses at force and injustice and to laugh at prisons and chains:

"I'll keep you bound
Both hand and foot, in savage custody."
—"Whene'er I please, a god will set me free."
I think he meant: I'll die. For death is final.

HORACE

Our religion has no surer human foundation than contempt for life. Not only do the arguments of reason invite us to it; for why should we fear to lose a thing which once lost cannot be regretted? And since we are threatened by so many kinds of death, is there not more pain in fearing them all than in enduring one?

What does it matter when it comes, since it is inevitable? To the man who told Socrates, "The thirty tyrants have condemned you to death," he replied: "And nature, them."

What stupidity to torment ourselves about passing into exemption from all torment! As our birth brought us the birth of all things, so will our death bring us the death of all things. Wherefore it is as foolish to lament that we shall not be alive a hundred years from now as it is to lament that we were not alive a hundred years ago. Death is the origin of another life. Just so did we weep, just so did we struggle against entering this life, just so did we strip off our former veil when we entered it.

Nothing can be grievous that happens only once. Is it reasonable so long to fear a thing so short? Long life and short life are made all one by death. For there is no long or short for things that are no more. Aristotle says that there are little animals by the river Hypanis that live only a day. The one that dies at eight o'clock in the morning dies in its youth; the one that dies at five in the afternoon dies in its decrepitude. Which of us does not laugh to see this moment of duration considered in terms of happiness or unhappiness? The length or shortness of our duration, if we compare it with eternity, or yet with the duration of mountains, rivers, stars, trees, and even of some animals, is no less ridiculous.

But Nature forces us to it. Go out of this world, she says, as you entered it. The same passage that you made from death to life, without feeling or fright, make it again from life to death. Your death is a part of the order of the universe; it is a part of the life of the world.

Our lives we borrow from each other . . .
And men, like runners, pass along the torch of life.

LUCRETIUS

Shall I change for you this beautiful contexture of things? Death is the condition of your creation, it is a part of you; you are fleeing from your own selves. This being of yours that you enjoy is equally divided between death and life. The first day of our birth leads you toward death as toward life:

The hour which gave us life led to its end.

SENECA

Even in birth we die; the end is there from the start.

MANILIUS

All the time you live you steal from life; living is at life's expense. The constant work of your life is to build death. You are in death while you are in life; for you are after death when you are no longer in life. Or, if you prefer it this way, you are dead after life; but during life you are dying; and death affects the dying much more roughly than the dead, and more keenly and essentially.

If you have made your profit of life, you have had your fill of it; go your way satisfied:

Why, like a well-filled guest, not leave the feast of life?

LUCRETIUS

If you have not known how to make good use of it, if it was useless to you, what do you care that you have lost it, what do you still want it for?

Why do you seek to add more years
Which too would pass but ill, and vanish unawares?

LUCRETIUS

Life is neither good nor evil in itself: it is the scene of good and evil according as you give them room.

And if you have lived a day, you have seen everything. One day is equal to all days. There is no other light, no other night. This sun, this moon, these stars, the way they are arranged, all is the very same your ancestors enjoyed and that will entertain your grandchildren:

Your ancestors beheld no other one, nor shall
Your nephews see another.

MANILIUS

And at worst, the distribution and variety of all the acts of my comedy runs its course in a year. If you have taken note of the revolution of my four seasons, they embrace the infancy, the youth, the manhood, and the old age of the world. It has played its part. It knows no other trick than to begin again. It will always be just this:

We turn in the same circle, and never leave;

LUCRETIUS

And on itself the year revolves along its track.

VIRGIL

I am not minded to make you any other new pastimes:

I can contrive, to please you, nothing more;

All things remain as they have been before.

LUCRETIUS

Make room for others, as others have for you. Equality is the principal part of equity. Who can complain of being included where all are included? And so, live as long as you please, you will strike nothing off the time you will have to spend dead; it is no use; you shall be as long in that state which you fear as if you had died nursing:

> So live victorious, live long as you will,
> Eternal death shall be there waiting still.

LUCRETIUS

And furthermore, I shall put you in such a condition as will give you no cause for complaint:

> Do you not know that when death comes, there'll be
> No other you to mourn your memory,
> And stand above you prostrate?

LUCRETIUS

Nor will you wish for the life you now lament so much:

> Then none shall mourn their person or their life . . .
> And all regret of self shall cease to be.

LUCRETIUS

Death is to be feared less than nothing, if there is anything less than nothing:

> For us far less a thing must death be thought,
> If ought there be that can be less than nought.

LUCRETIUS

It does not concern you dead or alive: alive, because you are; dead, because you are no more.

No one dies before his time. The time you leave behind was no more yours than that which passed before your birth, and it concerns you no more.

> Look back and see how past eternities of time
> Are nothing to us.

LUCRETIUS

Wherever your life ends, it is all there. The advantage of living is not measured by length, but by use; some men have lived long, and lived little; attend to it while you are in it. It lies in your will, not in the number of years, for you to have lived enough. Did you think you would never

arrive where you never ceased going? Yet there is no road but has its
end. And if company can comfort you, does not the world keep pace
with you?

All things, their life being done, will follow you.

LUCRETIUS

Does not everything move with your movement? Is there anything
that does not grow old along with you? A thousand men, a thousand
animals, and a thousand other creatures die at the very moment when
you die:

No night has ever followed day, no day the night,
That has not heard, amid the newborn infants' squalls,
The wild laments that go with death and funerals.

LUCRETIUS

Why do you recoil, if you cannot draw back? You have seen enough
men who were better off for dying, thereby avoiding great miseries.
Have you found any man that was worse off? How simple-minded it is
to condemn a thing that you have not experienced yourself or through
anyone else. Why do you complain of me and of destiny? Do we wrong
you? Is it for you to govern us, or us you? Though your age is not
full-grown, your life is. A little man is a whole man, just like a big one.
Neither men nor their lives are measured by the ell.

Chiron refused immortality when informed of its conditions by the
very god of time and duration, his father Saturn. Imagine honestly how
much less bearable and more painful to man would be an everlasting life
than the life I have given him. If you did not have death, you would
curse me incessantly for having deprived you of it. I have deliberately
mixed with it a little bitterness to keep you, seeing the convenience of it,
from embracing it too greedily and intemperately. To lodge you in that
moderate state that I ask of you, of neither fleeing life nor fleeing back
from death, I have tempered both of them between sweetness and
bitterness.

I taught Thales, the first of your sages, that life and death were
matters of indifference; wherefore, to the man who asked him why then
he did not die, he replied very wisely: "Because it is indifferent."

Water, earth, air, fire, and the other parts of this structure of mind are
no more instruments of your life than instruments of your death. Why
do you fear your last day? It contributes no more to your death than
each of the others. The last step does not cause fatigue, but reveals it. All
days travel toward death, the last one reaches it.

Such are the good counsels of our mother Nature. Now I have often pondered how it happens that in wars the face of death, whether we see it in ourselves or in others, seems to us incomparably less terrifying than in our houses—otherwise you would have an army of doctors and snivelers—and, since death is always the same, why nevertheless there is much more assurance against it among villagers and humble folk than among others. I truly think it is those dreadful faces and trappings with which we surround it, that frighten us more than death itself: an entirely new way of living; the cries of mothers, wives, and children; the visits of people dazed and benumbed by grief; the presence of a number of pale and weeping servants; a darkened room; lighted candles; our bedside beseiged by doctors and preachers; in short, everything horror and fright around us. There we are already shrouded and buried. Children fear even their friends when they see them masked, and so do we ours. We must strip the mask from things as well as from persons; when it is off, we shall find beneath only that same death which a valet or a mere chambermaid passed through not long ago without fear. Happy the death that leaves no leisure for preparing such ceremonies!